GRAMMARWORK

3

PAMELA BREYER

ENGLISH EXERCISES IN CONTEXT

Prentice Hall Regents, Englewood Cliffs, NJ 07632

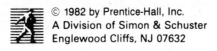 © 1982 by Prentice-Hall, Inc.
A Division of Simon & Schuster
Englewood Cliffs, NJ 07632

Book Design: **Suzanne Bennett & Associates**
CREDITS: Page 1, photo courtesy of Ethan Allen, Inc.
Pages 2, 8, 18, 56, 70, 71, 74, 81, 84, 90, 93, 97, 101,
illustrations by Erasmo Hernandez. Page 3, photo
courtesy of H.U.D. Pages 4, 5, 6, 7, 10, 19, 31, 49, 51, 52,
53, 62, 68, 76, 79, 87, 98, illustrations by Ellen Eagle.
Pages 5, 9, 11, 13, 17, 25, 28, 30, 43, 45, 47, 67, 71, 78, 89,
96, 103, illustrations by Anne Burgess. Pages 22, 26, 36,
40, 66, 105, photos by Rick Maiman. Page 60, illus-
tration by Anna Veltfort. Page 80, symbols courtesy of
A. T. & T. Co.

Printed in the United States of America

10   9   8   7   6   5

ISBN 0-13-362294-0

Prentice-Hall International (UK) Limited, *London*
Prentice-Hall of Australia Pty. Limited, *Sydney*
Prentice-Hall Canada Inc., *Toronto*
Prentice-Hall Hispanoamericana, S.A., *Mexico*
Prentice-Hall of India Private Limited, *New Delhi*
Prentice-Hall of Japan, Inc., *Tokyo*
Simon & Schuster Asia Pte. Ltd., *Singapore*
Editora Prentice-Hall do Brasil, Ltda., *Rio de Janeiro*

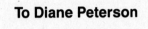

To Diane Peterson

Contents

Introduction

Many teachers believe that students acquire and retain a new language more rapidly and more efficiently when the structure and vocabulary of the language are presented in contexts; that is, when elements of a lesson such as grammar and lexicon are tied together in a real and meaningful setting. Exercises which do this—present material in a situational context—are referred to as contextualized exercises.

GrammarWork is a series of four contextualized exercise books for students of written English. These books may be used as major text or supplementary material, depending on whether a course is non-intensive or intensive, with any notional-functional or grammar-oriented syllabus. Each exercise presents vocabulary relating to a particular context and structures that are appropriate to that context together as a unit, rather than as isolated language fragments.

Book One is intended for the beginner: the student enrolled in a first-level English course with some exposure to the language. Book Two continues with beginners' material, proceeding from first-level to second-level work. Book Three is designed for the intermediate student, and Book Four is essentially a review of the first three books, adding occasional new material appropriate to intermediate levels. Book Four, particularly, was designed for both the native and the non-native student of English.

The exercises in each book are, for the most part, divided into three sections: 1) An examination of the structure to be presented ("Grammar"); 2) Exercises which enable the student to manipulate that new structure in a contextual setting ("Practice"); 3) A culminating exercise activity in which the student uses the material in the exercise by applying it to a personal, real-life situation ("Make It Work").

The Grammar section shows the student how to use the structure to be practiced, with diagrams and arrows that should be self-explanatory. Notes of explanation are supplied only when the grammar rule cannot be illustrated sufficiently.

Closely related to the GrammarWork exercises is an extensive grammar reference work, GrammarGuide by Janet Bing. This book explains and illustrates with examples the GrammarWork exercise items. The numbers at the beginning of each Grammar section in GrammarWork are coordinated with the GrammarGuide reference. For example, the number 2.13 under the heading Possessive of Nouns in the workbook indicates that a more comprehensive grammatical explanation of noun possessives is to be found in Chapter 2, item 13 of the reference book.

The Practice section consists of the contextualized exercises, usually a page in length and always self-contained; if a context is three pages instead of one, it will be self-contained within those three pages. Thus the teacher can select any exercise or group of exercises considered appropriate for a particular class or lesson and can also feel free to use only those exercises considered useful at a given time.

However, the teacher can also choose to utilize all the exercises in the order presented; the exercises have been written and arranged in ascending order of difficulty, with structures generally considered to be the easiest for most students to learn presented first.

The exercises are "self-contained" in that they have been designed for written practice without necessarily being preceded by an introductory teachers' presentation. Since grammatical explanations have been included and the new vocabulary is usually illustrated or defined, students can work independently, either at home or in class—in pairs or as a group. When students work together in pairs or in groups in the classroom, they should be encouraged to help each other; the teacher, too, can assist by circulating from pair to pair or group to group, guiding and correcting.

The Make It Work section enables students to apply what they have been practicing to freer, sometimes more natural situations. The activity usually contains a picture cue, a fill-in dialogue, or questions to answer. The purpose of Make It Work is to have the student experience the material in as close to a real-life setting as possible.

The perforated answer key can be used by either the student or the teacher. The teacher may choose to withhold the answers on some occasions; on other occasions, the students may be permitted to have access to the answer key for self-correcting purposes.

Acknowledgments

No book of this kind can be written without a great deal of help, at every step of the way, from both colleagues and friends. In particular, I would like to thank:

Gary Gabriel, my former teacher at Teachers College, Columbia University, whose help and encouragement brought me into the field of E.S.L. in New York and whose ideas have guided the philosophy behind this series.

David Tillyer, my editor at Regents Publishing Company, for sharing ideas which have helped to shape these books.

Gloria Gallingane, LaGuardia Community College, and Janet Bing for their suggestions and support during the writing of these books.

P.B.

Cars are expensive.

NO ARTICLE WITH GENERAL STATEMENTS
VERB *TO BE*

GrammarGuide
2.9

A car costs $6,000.	Cars	**are expensive.**
A couch costs $650.	Couches	**are expensive.**

Note: **You can make a general statement about a whole class of things by using the plural form of countable nouns. For general statements, do not use *the* before the plural form.**

Add *s* to form the regular plural: house–houses

Add *s* to words ending in vowel + *o*: radio–radios

Add *es* to words ending in *s*, *sh*, *ch*, *x*, and *z*:
couch–couches   dish–dishes

Practice

Make general plural sentences.

1. A house costs $80,000.

2. A car costs $6,000.

3. A television costs $400.

4. A washing machine costs $350.

5. A clothes dryer costs $400.

6. A refrigerator costs $700.

7. A stereo costs $800.

8. A dishwasher costs $500.

9. A stove costs $800.

10. A bed costs $500.

11. A rug costs $350.

12. A couch costs $650.

Houses are expensive.

_____

_____

_____

_____

_____

_____

_____

_____

_____

_____

_____

Make It Work

Name three other household items that are expensive.

Desks are expensive.

_____

_____

_____

1

Tables and chairs are in the furniture department.

COMPOUND SUBJECTS
VERB *TO BE*

GrammarGuide
10.2

DIRECTORY	
HOUSEWARE DEPARTMENT:	spoons, dishes, pans, plates
APPLIANCE DEPARTMENT:	televisions, refrigerators, washing machines, clothes dryers
FURNITURE DEPARTMENT:	tables, chairs, couches, dressers
BEDDING DEPARTMENT:	sheets, blankets, pillow cases
BATH DEPARTMENT:	towels, wash cloths, bath mats, shower curtains

Refrigerators and stoves are in the appliance department.

 Practice

Tell where to find the following things.

1. I want to buy a refrigerator.
   I want to buy a stove.

   Refrigerators and stoves are in the appliance department.

2. I want to buy a serving dish.
   I want to buy a salad bowl.

3. I want to buy a dresser.
   I want to buy a chair.

4. I want to buy a shower curtain.
   I want to buy a bath mat.

5. I want to buy a sheet.
   I want to buy a blanket.

6. I want to buy a couch.
   I want to buy a coffee table.

7. I want to buy a pot.
   I want to buy a pan.

8. I want to buy a towel.
   I want to buy a wash cloth.

9. I want to buy a television.
   I want to buy a stereo.

10. I want to buy a table.
    I want to buy a chair.

11. I want to buy a pillow case.
    I want to buy a sheet.

12. I want to buy a washing machine.
    I want to buy a clothes dryer.

All the homes are 2,000 square feet.

NOUN PLURALS: REGULAR AND IRREGULAR

VERB *TO BE*

GrammarGuide
2.3

–s/–es	–ies	–ves	Irregular
bath–bath $\boxed{\text{s}}$	study–stud $\boxed{\text{ies}}$	shelf–shel $\boxed{\text{ves}}$	foot– $\boxed{\text{feet}}$
room–room $\boxed{\text{s}}$		knife–kni $\boxed{\text{ves}}$	
box–box $\boxed{\text{es}}$		**Spelling exception:**	
patio–patio $\boxed{\text{s}}$		roof–roofs	

Practice

Fill in the blanks with the correct plural form.

Windy Bush is an elegant development of fine homes. All the homes in the

development are 2,000 square _____feet_____ with two and a half
(1. foot)

_____ and four _____ . All houses have plaster
(2. bath)   (3. bedroom)

_____ , wooden _____ , _____ , two-car
(4. wall)   (5. roof)   (6. patio)

_____ , and two _____ . Some models have extra
(7. garage)   (8. fireplace)

_____ or _____ . These beautiful homes have built-in
(9. den)   (10. study)

_____ , deluxe _____ , built-in _____ on three
(11. bookshelf)   (12. oven)   (13. window box)

windows, built-in _____ in all kitchens, and wooden _____
(14. radio)   (15. floor)

throughout each house.

Equivalent:

square foot = .09 meter^2

New Words:

plaster–a mixture used on walls to give a smooth surface
wooden–made of wood
built-in–a part of something that cannot be separated from it

Sharks are dangerous.

Fish

a shark

a goldfish

Birds

a goose

a pigeon

a parrot

Reptiles

a snake

an alligator

a turtle

Rodents

a mouse

a rat

Insects

a scorpion

an ant

a moth

a butterfly

Sharks are dangerous.

NOUN PLURALS: REGULAR AND IRREGULAR
VERB *TO BE*

GrammarGuide
2.3

| Rattlesnakes | are dangerous. |

| Mice | aren't dangerous. |

Note: Irregular Plurals:
      mouse–mice
      goose–geese

Singular and plural forms are the same:
      deer–deer
      sheep–sheep
      fish–fish

Practice

Look at page 4. Then make the sentences plural.

1. A shark is dangerous.   Sharks are dangerous.

2. A goldfish isn't dangerous.

3. A rattlesnake is dangerous.

4. An alligator is dangerous.

5. A pigeon isn't dangerous.

6. A goose isn't dangerous.

7. A mouse isn't dangerous.

8. A rat is dangerous.

9. A deer isn't dangerous.

10. A horse isn't dangerous.

11. A sheep isn't dangerous.

12. A wasp is dangerous.

Make It Work

Name one kind of insect you're afraid of.   I'm afraid of wasps.

Name one kind of fish you're afraid of.

Name one kind of reptile you're afraid of.

New Words:

 deer   **sheep**

A moth is an insect.

ARTICLES *A* AND *AN* FOR CLASSIFYING STATEMENTS
VERB *TO BE*

GrammarGuide
2.7

| A | butterfly is | an | insect. |

| An | alligator is | a | reptile. |

| A | mouse is | a | rodent. |

Note: You can make a general statement about a whole class of things using *a* or *an* before the singular form of countable nouns.
See page 5 for irregular plurals.

Practice

Look at the pictures on page 4. Then make the sentences singular.

1. Pigeons are birds.   A pigeon is a bird.

2. Sharks are fish.   _____

3. Snakes are reptiles.   _____

4. Butterflies are insects. _____

5. Geese are birds.   _____

6. Alligators are reptiles. _____

7. Wasps are insects.   _____

8. Parrots are birds.   _____

9. Mice are rodents.   _____

10. Flies are insects.   _____

11. Turtles are reptiles.   _____

12. Cockroaches are insects. _____

13. Rats are rodents.   _____

14. Ants are insects.   _____

15. Goldfish are fish.   _____

Make it Work

Fill in the blanks.

_____ is a beautiful bird.
_____ is a beautiful insect.
_____ is a beautiful fish.

The garden tools are on special.

NOUNS IN ADJECTIVE POSITION
VERB *TO BE*

GrammarGuide
2.14

roses   bushes | rose | bushes

Note: Don't add *s* or *es* to nouns used in adjective position.

Practice

Put the words in parentheses in adjective position.

1. Which plants are on sale today? (tomato)   the tomato plants _____

2. Which pots are on sale? (flower)   _____

3. Which bushes are reduced? (rose)   _____

4. Which tools are on special? (garden)   _____

5. Which chairs are on sale? (beach)   _____

6. Which brushes are on special? (paint)   _____

7. Which bowls are reduced? (salad)   _____

8. Which tables are on sale? (coffee)   _____

9. Which curtains are on special? (shower)   _____

10. Which supplies are reduced? (office)   _____

11. Which frames are on special? (picture)   _____

12. Which clocks are reduced? (wall)   _____

Make It Work

Read the dialogue. Then write a dialogue about books.

- ■ Are the birthday cards on sale?   _____?
- ☐ No, they aren't.   _____.
- ■ Which cards are on sale?   _____?
- ☐ The Christmas cards.   _____.
- ■ Thank you.   _____.

The others are made of silk.

ANOTHER, *THE OTHER*, AND *THE OTHERS*
VERB *TO BE*

GrammarGuide
3.9

One tie is made of cotton.

| The other ties | are made of silk. |
| The others | are made of silk. |

Four ties are made of silk.

| The other tie | is made of cotton. |
| The other | is made of cotton. |

Two ties are $12.95.

| Another tie | is $15.50. |
| Another | is $15.50. |

Note: the others = the only ones left
the other = the only one left
another = one of several (singular)

 Practice

Look at the picture above. Then fill in the blanks with *another*, *the other*, or *the others*.
Use the words *tie* or *ties* when necessary.

Two ties are less than $15.00.

1. The other ties are more than $15.00.

2. The others are more than $15.00.

Two ties are $12.95.

3. _____ _____ is $16.95.

4. _____ is $16.95.

Four ties need to be dry cleaned.

5. _____ _____ _____ is washable.

6. _____ _____ is washable.

Two ties are narrow.

7. _____ _____ _____ are wide.

8. _____ _____ are wide.

One tie is striped.

9. _____ _____ is plaid.

10. _____ is plaid.

The kitchen isn't large enough.

TOO** AND **NOT...ENOUGH

VERB *TO BE*

GrammarGuide
8.7

> The closet is small.
>
> The closet is | too | small.
>
> The closet is | n't | large | enough.

Note: Place *too* before adjectives. Place *enough* after adjectives.

Practice

Add *too* or *enough* to the sentences.

1. My apartment is expensive. (too)   <u>My apartment is too expensive.</u>

2. My apartment is also small. (too)

3. It isn't spacious, either. (enough)

4. The kitchen isn't large. (enough)

5. There's one closet in the apartment, and it's small. (too)

6. It isn't cool in the summer. (enough)

7. In the winter, it's cool. (too)

8. It isn't close to a shopping area. (enough)

9. And it's far from the bus station. (too)

10. My building isn't elegant on the outside. (enough)

11. My street isn't safe. (enough)

12. The neighborhood is dangerous. (too)

Make It Work

Tell four things wrong with your apartment or house.

My _____ is too _____ .

It isn't _____ .

_____ .

_____ .

New Word:

spacious—having a lot of room

9

She's too short to be on the basketball team.

***TOO* AND *ENOUGH* WITH INFINITIVES**
VERB *TO BE*

GrammarGuide
8.7

> She's ⬚too⬚ short ⬚to be⬚ on the basketball team.
>
> She is ⬚n't⬚ tall ⬚enough⬚ ⬚to be⬚ on the basketball team.

Practice

Make sentences with *too*, *enough*, and an infinitive.

She can't be on the basketball team.

1. short   She's too short to be on the basketball team.

2. tall   She isn't tall enough to be on the basketball team.

He can't play on the football team.

3. small   _____

4. big   _____

5. heavy   _____

6. light   _____

She can't run on the track team.

7. fast   _____

8. slow   _____

He can't play professional baseball.

9. young   _____

10. old   _____

Make It Work

Look at the dialogue. Then fill in the blank.

■ How about a game of tennis this afternoon?

☐ It's 95 degrees today.
It's too hot to play tennis.

■ Let's go swimming this afternoon.

☐ It's 40 degrees today.

_____ .

New Words:

team–a group of people who play a sport together
track (team)–racing or running (team)
professional–making money by playing a sport

Equivalents:

95 degrees F. = 35 degrees C.
40 degrees F. = 4 degrees C.

10

There are a lot of tall buildings in a big city.

AFFIRMATIVE STATEMENTS WITH *A LOT OF*
THERE IS AND *THERE ARE*

GrammarGuide
7.4

There are a lot of   tall buildings in a big city.

There's a lot of   traffic in a big city.

Note: Use *a lot of* with both countable and uncountable nouns.
Use *there is* with uncountable nouns:

traffic	industry
air pollution	crime
litter	noise

 Practice

Make sentences about a big city. Use *there's* or *there are* and *a lot of.*

1. industry   There's a lot of industry _____ in a big city.
2. jobs _____ in a big city.
3. tall buildings _____ in a big city.
4. big department stores _____ in a big city.
5. museums _____ in a big city.
6. air pollution _____ in a big city.
7. litter _____ in a big city.
8. factories _____ in a big city.
9. noise _____ in a big city.
10. traffic _____ in a big city.
11. crime _____ in a big city.
12. robberies _____ in a big city.

 Make It Work

Give two reasons to live in a big city.
There _____ . There _____ .
Give two reasons not to live in a big city.
_____ . _____ .

New Words:

industry–large business
air pollution–air that is not clean or pure
factory–a building where things are made

litter–trash on the street
crime–robberies, murders

11

There isn't much traffic in a small town.

NEGATIVE STATEMENTS WITH *MUCH* AND *MANY*

THERE IS* AND *THERE ARE

GrammarGuide
7.4

> There are a lot of people in a big city.
>
> There aren't | many | people in a small town.
>
> There's a lot of industry in a big city.
>
> There isn't | much | industry in a small town.
>
> **Note:** Use ***much*** with uncountable nouns and ***many*** with countable nouns.

Practice

Make sentences about a small town. Use *there isn't (aren't)* and *much* or *many*.

1. tall buildings   There aren't many tall buildings _____ in a small town.
2. traffic   _____ in a small town.
3. highways   _____ in a small town.
4. supermarkets   _____ in a small town.
5. restaurants   _____ in a small town.
6. noise at night   _____ in a small town.
7. crime   _____ in a small town.
8. apartment buildings _____ in a small town.
9. industry   _____ in a small town.
10. department stores _____ in a small town.
11. air pollution   _____ in a small town.
12. factories   _____ in a small town.

Make It Work

Tell about your city or town.

There are a lot of _____ in _____ .

There isn't much _____

There aren't many _____

_____

_____

There are no factories in Titusville.

NEGATIVE STATEMENTS WITH *NO*
THERE IS* AND *THERE ARE

GrammarGuide
7.4

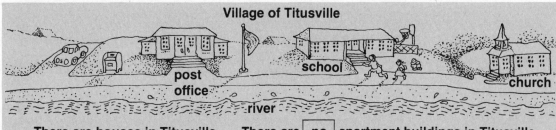

Village of Titusville

post office

school

church

river

There are houses in Titusville.   There are no apartment buildings in Titusville.

Note: When you put *no* before a noun, it expresses a negative idea.
There are no bars = There aren't any bars.

Practice

Make negative statements about the village of Titusville.

1. factories   There are no factories in Titusville.

2. industry   _____

3. air pollution   _____

4. department stores _____

5. shops   _____

6. supermarkets   _____

7. activity at night _____

8. highways   _____

9. traffic   _____

10. apartment buildings _____

11. hotels   _____

12. noise at night   _____

13. restaurants   _____

14. bars   _____

15. movie theaters   _____

They're working for their father now.

NEGATIVE AND AFFIRMATIVE STATEMENTS
PRESENT CONTINUOUS

GrammarGuide
4.5
4.2

Tina	**is teaching**	now.
Dave and his brother	**are working**	for their father now.
Patty	**isn't working**	now.
Bill and his wife	**aren't working**	now.

work-working study-studying	live-living make-making	sit-sitting put-putting
Note: Add *ing* to the simple form of the verb.	If a verb ends in consonant + e, omit the e and add *ing*.	Double the consonant before adding *ing* to one-syllable verbs ending in consonant. Do not double w, x, or y.

Practice

Tina meets Bev in a department store, and they talk about what their high school friends are doing.

Fill in the blanks with the correct form of the present continuous. Use contractions with pronouns.

Bev: Tina Palaferri!

Tina: Bev Smith. I can't believe it! How are you?

Bev: I'm fine. I __'m__ ___working___ in a bank now. What are you doing?
        (1. work)

Tina: I ____ _____ now.
            (2. teach)

Bev: How about LuEllen? What's she doing?

Tina: I'm not sure. I think she ____ _____ to school.
                    (3. go)

Bev: Do you remember Mary Lu?

Tina: Yes, of course.

Bev: Her husband ____ _____ a novel.
                (4. write)

Tina: What about Patty?

Bev: She ____ _____ . She and her husband
            (5. not/work)

____ _____ a new house in Laguna Beach.
        (6. build)

14

Tina: How are Dave Robertson and his brother Mike?

Bev: They _____ _____ very well. They _____ _____ for
(7. do)   (8. work)

their father now. What's Linda Lee doing?

Tina: She _____ _____ at the university.
(9. study)

She _____ _____ on her degree in English.
(10. work)

Bev: I think Inez Naples _____ _____ a degree in history. How are
(11. get)

Sue and Tom O'Connor?

Tina: They _____ _____ in Texas now.
(12. live)

They _____ _____ for a real estate company.
(13. work)

Tom _____ _____ houses, and Sue _____ _____
(14. build)   (15. sell)

them.

Bev: What's Tom's brother Bill doing?

Tina: He and his wife _____ _____ in New York.
(16. live)

They _____ _____ very well. Bill _____ _____
(17. not/do)   (18. not/work)

now, and his wife _____ _____ for a job. I think
(19. look)

they _____ _____ a divorce.
(20. get)

Bev: I'm sorry to hear that. Well, I have to go now. It's great to see you.

Tina: Good to see you too. Bye.

Make It Work

Tell about two of your school friends.

Sherry Jacobs is working for a travel agency.

_____

_____

New Words:

degree–an award for achievement in a college or university
real estate company–a business that sells land and houses
divorce–the ending of a marriage by a court

Is she still looking for a job?

YES-NO QUESTIONS

PRESENT CONTINUOUS

GrammarGuide
4.2

> **Bev is living in Costa Mesa.**
>
> **Is Bev still working in a bank?**
>
> **Dave and Mike Robertson are living in Newport Beach.**
>
> **Are Dave and Mike Robertson still working for their father?**

 ## Practice

It is one year later.
Look at pages 14 and 15. Then ask questions about the following people. Use *still*.

1. Bev   Is Bev still working _____ in a bank?

2. Tina   _____ ?

3. LuEllen   _____ to school?

4. Patty and her
   husband   _____ a house?

5. Mary Lu's husband _____ a novel?

6. Dave and Mike
   Robertson   _____ for their father?

7. Linda Lee   _____ at the university?

8. Sue and Tom
   O'Connor   _____ in Texas?

9. Tom O'Connor   _____ houses?

10. Sue O'Connor   _____ houses?

11. Bill O'Connor   _____ in New York?

12. Bill O'Connor's wife _____ for a job?

 ## Make It Work

Look at the dialogue. Then write a dialogue about a school friend you know.

- ■ How's Jim Carson?
- ☐ Oh, fine. He's living in San Diego now.

- ■ Is he still studying to be a doctor?

- ☐ Yes, I think so.

- ■ How's _____ ?
- ☐ Oh, fine. _____ _____ now.

- ■ _____ ?

- ☐ Yes, I think so.

16

He drives trucks.

AFFIRMATIVE STATEMENTS WITH *HE* AND *SHE*

SIMPLE PRESENT

GrammarGuide
4.4

What does an elevator operator do?

She │ operates │ elevators.

What does a window washer do?

She │ washes │ windows.

What does a truck driver do?

He │ drives │ trucks.

Note: Add *s* to the simple form of the verb.
Add *es* when verbs end in *s*, *sh*, *ch*, *x*, or *z*.
Add *s* to verbs that end in e:
    drive   operate
    produce   tune
    make

 Practice

Tell what the following people do for a living.

1. What does an elevator operator do?   She <u>operates elevators.</u>

2. What does a movie producer do?   She _____

3. What does a taxi driver do?   He _____

4. What does a window washer do?   She _____

5. What does a dressmaker do?   She _____

6. What does a switchboard operator do?   She _____

7. What does an animal trainer do?   He _____

8. What does a book publisher do?   He _____

9. What does a truck driver do?   She _____

10. What does a shoemaker do?   He _____

11. What does a house painter do?   He _____

12. What does a bookkeeper do?   She _____

13. What does a dog catcher do?   He _____

14. What does a piano tuner do?   She _____

15. What does a street cleaner do?   He _____

17

She doesn't answer the telephone.

NEGATIVE AND AFFIRMATIVE STATEMENTS
SIMPLE PRESENT

GrammarGuide
4.2
4.4

| She doesn't | answer | the telephone. |
| Her maid | answers | the telephone. |

Practice

Fill in the blanks with the correct form of the verb.

Marie Moreau is a very famous and very rich person.

1. (get) She doesn't _____ get _____ up early in the morning.

2. (get) She _____ up whenever she wants to.

3. (clean) She doesn't _____ her house.

4. (clean) Her cleaning woman _____ her house.

5. (fix) She doesn't _____ her own breakfast.

6. (fix) Her maid _____ breakfast for her.

7. (answer) When the doorbell rings, she doesn't _____ the door.

8. (answer) Her butler _____ the door.

9. (get) She doesn't _____ dressed by herself.

10. (help) Her maid _____ her get dressed.

11. (answer) If the telephone rings, she doesn't _____ it.

12. (answer) Her maid _____ the telephone.

Make It Work

Look at the advertisement. Then fill in the blanks.

```
* * * * * * * * * * * * *
*                       *
*   PETE'S  AUTO        *
*                       *
*      REPAIR           *
*  TRAINED * MECHANICS  *
*  DOMESTIC  CARS       *
*                       *
*      875 - 6601       *
* * * * * * * * * * * * *
```

Pete's doesn't _____ foreign cars.

It only _____ domestic cars.

New Word:

butler—a man who works as a servant in another person's house

18

Their jobs require a lot of accuracy.

NEGATIVE AND AFFIRMATIVE STATEMENTS WITH *THEY*

SIMPLE PRESENT

GrammarGuide
4.2
4.4

Charlie works in a bank.

Charlie and Roger | work | **in a bank.**

Practice

Write about Charlie and Roger instead of Charlie. You will be writing about two people. Change *his* and *him* to *their* and *them*.

1. Charlie works in a bank.

2. He's a teller who handles a lot of money every day.

3. He cashes checks for people.

4. He adds figures, and he counts money.

5. He counts everything twice so that he doesn't make mistakes.

6. His job requires a lot of accuracy.

7. He also has to be fast at what he does.

8. He receives and pays out hundreds of dollars every hour.

9. He smiles at all the customers.

10. He enjoys his job very much.

11. But there's one thing that worries him.

12. He's afraid of bank robbers.

Charlie and Roger work in a bank.

They're tellers who _____

New Words:

accuracy—being careful or correct
twice—two times

19

It's the first house on the right.

PREPOSITIONS OF PLACE

GrammarGuide
9.2

I live	at	56 Royal Lane.
	on	Royal Lane
	on	the corner of Royal Lane and High Street
	on	the right side of the street
	in	an apartment
	in	Dallas

Practice

Fill in the blanks with *in, on,* or *at.*

1. I live __on__ Royal Lane __in__ North Dallas.

2. It's the first house _____ the right.

3. I live _____ 52 Main Street.

4. That's _____ Houston.

5. I live _____ Century Village _____ apartment 63-C.

6. It's the third building _____ the left.

7. My address is 412 Main Street _____ Dallas.

8. I live _____ the top floor _____ apartment 10-F.

9. I live _____ Silverton _____ the corner of Union Street and Fourth Avenue.

10. I live _____ 16 Park Place, apartment 1-B.

11. It's the second door _____ your right.

12. I live _____ Windy Bush _____ 5236 Brook Drive.

Make It Work

Read the telephone message. Then write a telephone report of a fire in your kitchen.

This is an emergency.

There's a robber in my apartment.

I live at 2576 High Street in Dallas.

Please come immediately.

This is _____

There's _____

_____

Please come immediately.

New Word:

emergency—an unexpected event which you must do something about at once

20

It's cheaper to travel in February.

PREPOSITIONS OF TIME

SIMPLE PRESENT

GrammarGuide
9.3

The plane arrives	at	5:00	in	the evening	on	Saturday
	at	noon	in	the morning	on	February 13th
	at	night	in	January	on	the weekend

Practice

Fill in the dialogue with *in, on,* or *at.*

Chang: I want a plane ticket from New York to Los Angeles sometime

___in___ March.
(1.)

Travel Agent: It's cheaper to travel _____ February. There are reduced fares
(2.)

_____ January and February, but not _____ Washington's Birthday.
(3.)   (4.)

Chang: O.K. Do you have a flight _____ February 13th?
(5.)

Travel Agent: I think so. That's _____ a Saturday. There's a plane to Los Angeles
(6.)

_____ noon. It gets there _____ 3:00 _____ the afternoon, Los
(7.)   (8.)   (9.)

Angeles time.

Chang: How much does that cost?

Travel Agent: It's $485.00, round trip.

Chang: Do you have anything cheaper?

Travel Agent: Yes, but not _____ the weekend. We have a flight to Los Angeles
(10.)

_____ the evening _____ Thursday. It arrives _____ 2:30 a.m.
(11.)   (12.)   (13.)

_____ Friday.
(14.)

Chang: How much is that?

Travel Agent: The fare is cheaper _____ night. It's $265.00.
(15.)

Chang: That sounds fine. I'd like to make a reservation.

New Words:

a.m.—before 12:00 noon and after 12:00 midnight   **fare—the price for transportation**
p.m.—after 12:00 noon and before 12:00 midnight   **round trip—a trip to a place and back**

21

What time on Sunday does she arrive?

SIMPLE PRESENT WITH FUTURE MEANING

QUESTIONS WITH *WHAT TIME*

GrammarGuide
4.4
3.7

What time	does she arrive?
	She arrives at 5:50.
What time	do they arrive?
	They arrive at 5:20.

Practice

Make questions with *what time*.

1. We arrive on February 13th.

   What time on February 13th do you arrive?

2. He arrives in the evening.

3. They leave on Friday.

4. It leaves on Wednesday.

5. She arrives on March 18th.

6. We arrive in the morning.

7. I arrive on February 6th.

8. They arrive on Sunday.

9. We leave on the 9th.

10. It arrives in the morning.

11. They leave on September 6th.

12. He leaves in the afternoon.

Make It Work

Fill in the dialogues. Make questions with *what time*.

■ Can you take me to the airport? I leave next Tuesday.

□ What time _____ ?

■ Can you pick my brother up at the train station? He arrives Saturday afternoon.

□ _____ ?

22

He wants to get a job.

VERB + INFINITIVE

SIMPLE PRESENT, PRESENT CONTINUOUS

GrammarGuide
6.4

> **He wants** to come **to New York.**
>
> **Note: Use** *to* **+ the simple form of the verb after these verbs:**
>
> hope   refuse   need   expect   afford   want

 Practice

Fill in the blanks with an appropriate verb.

1. Roger McIntyre is a waiter, but he wants ____to be____ an actor.

2. He hopes _____ a big Broadway star.

3. He expects _____ to New York next fall.

4. But he needs _____ $183.92 for his bus trip.

5. He can't afford _____ by plane, so he's going by bus.

6. He wants _____ a job when he arrives in New York.

7. He doesn't expect _____ a job on Broadway right away.

8. He knows that he needs _____ hard to get a job on Broadway.

9. He hopes _____ a famous actor.

10. He refuses _____ his dream.
    (give up)

 Make It Work

Complete the sentences about yourself. Use negative or affirmative verbs from the
PRACTICE above.

I _____ get a better job.

_____ work hard.

_____ earn a lot of money someday.

New Words:
refuse–not to do something
afford–be able to buy
star–a famous performer
Broadway–a street in New York City with a lot of theaters
dream–something not real but believed in greatly

23

I don't enjoy being famous.

VERB + GERUND

SIMPLE PRESENT, PRESENT CONTINUOUS, *GOING-TO* FUTURE

GrammarGuide
6.4

I don't enjoy │ having │ my picture taken.

Note: Use the *ing* form of the verb after these verbs:

finish	can't help	keep on	imagine	enjoy
quit	avoid	appreciate	mind	

Practice

Fill in the blanks with the correct gerund form.

Interviewer: Hello everyone. I'm talking with Marie Moreau today. Marie, you're very

famous. Do you enjoy _____being_____ famous?
(1. be)

Marie: No, not really. People are always asking me for autographs.

Interviewer: Do you mind _____ autographs?
(2. sign)

Marie: No, I sign autographs everywhere I go.

Interviewer: Do you appreciate _____ letters from your fans?
(3. get)

Marie: No. I hate it.

Interviewer: What about photographers?

Marie: I can't help _____ my picture taken, but I avoid
(4. have)
_____ in public as much as possible.
(5. be)

Interviewer: What's your next movie?

Marie: It's not a movie. It's a play.

Interviewer: Are you going to quit _____ movies?
(6. make)

Marie: No, I can't imagine _____ anything else. I'm going to keep on
(7. do)
_____ movies.
(8. make)

Interviewer: What play are you going to be in?

Marie: "Little Children."

Interviewer: When do you finish _____ for it?
(9. rehearse)

Marie: Next month.

Interviewer: Well, good luck with your new play. I enjoyed _____ with you.
(10. talk)

New Words:

avoid–keep away from
appreciate–be thankful for
mind–be troubled by

keep on–continue
fan–a follower of a famous person
rehearse–practice for performance

24

She enjoys working. She wants to work.

VERB + GERUND VS. VERB + INFINITIVE
SIMPLE PRESENT, *GOING-TO* FUTURE

GrammarGuide
6.4

She wants | to work | as long as possible.
She enjoys | working.

Practice

Fill in the blanks with the correct form of the verb.

1. (work) Laura is expecting a baby. She wants _____to work_____ until the baby arrives.

2. (take) Then she expects _____ a leave of absence.

3. (work) She's going to quit _____ at the end of the month.

4. (go) After she has the baby, she hopes _____ back to work in a month.

5. (work) She's going to be a mother and she's going to keep on _____ at the same time.

6. (have) It's going to be hard, but she doesn't mind _____ two jobs.

7. (be) She wants _____ a mother.

8. (give up) But she refuses _____ her career as a lawyer.

9. (stay) Besides, she can't imagine _____ at home all the time.

10. (work) She enjoys _____.

11. (be) She's also going to enjoy _____ a mother.

12. (be) She hopes _____ a good lawyer and a good mother.

Make It Work

Complete the sentences about yourself.

I hope _____ .

I enjoy _____ .

I don't expect _____ .

New Word:

leave of absence–permission to be absent from work, usually for a long period of time

25

I don't know what she wants.

NOUN CLAUSES AS OBJECTS
VERB *TO BE*, SIMPLE PRESENT

GrammarGuide
2.19

	What does she need?
I don't know	**what** **she needs.**

	What's her favorite color?
I don't know	**what** **her favorite color is.**

Practice

Answer the questions. Begin with *I don't know, I'm not sure, I have no idea.*

1. It's Louise's birthday. What can we get her?

   I don't know what we can get her.

2. What does she need?

   I have no idea what she needs.

3. What does she want?

4. What's her favorite color?

5. What kind of book does she like?

6. What type of jewelry does she like?

7. What size glove does she wear?

8. What's her favorite perfume?

9. What kind of candy does she like?

10. What's her favorite flower?

Make It Work

You need to buy a gift for a male friend, but you don't know what to get him. Fill in the dialogue.

■ What does he need?

☐ I don't know what he needs.

■ What size does he wear?

☐ _____ , but I think it's a large.

26

Do you know how far it is?

NOUN CLAUSES AS OBJECTS
VERB *TO BE*, SIMPLE PRESENT, PRESENT CONTINUOUS

GrammarGuide
2.19

		What time does it start?
Do you know		**what time** it starts?

		How long is it?
Do you know		**how long** it is?

Note: Don't contract words with *is* at the end of a sentence.

Practice

You and your friend want to go to a new movie. Ask your friend questions about the movie. Fill in the blanks.

1. What movie is it?   Do you know <u>what movie it is?</u>

2. What time does it start?   Do you know _____

3. What time does the next show start?   Do you know _____

4. Where's it playing?   Do you know _____

5. Where's the Strand Theater?   Do you know _____

6. How far is it?   Do you know _____

7. How long does it take to get there?   Do you know _____

8. What time does it end?   Do you know _____

9. How long is it?   Do you know _____

10. How much does it cost?   Do you know _____

Make It Work

You are at a movie. Ask the person next to you the following questions.

Where's the nearest exit?   <u>Excuse me. Do you know where the nearest exit is?</u>

Where's the telephone?   _____

Where's the restroom?   _____

Where's the drinking fountain?   _____

27

A big bad wolf jumped out of the bushes.

A big bad wolf jumped out of the bushes.

SPELLING: REGULAR VERBS

SIMPLE PAST

GrammarGuide
4.14

-d/-ed	consonant + -ed
decide–decide d	stop–stop ped
walk–walk ed	shop–shop ped
Note: Add *d* or *ed* to form the past tense.	**Double the consonant before adding *ed* to one-syllable words ending in consonant + vowel + consonant.**

 Practice

Fill in the blanks with the correct past form.

Little Red Riding Hood _____lived_____ with her parents in a little house near the
(1. live)

forest. One day, Little Red Riding Hood _____ to visit her grandmother.
(2. decide)

She _____ some cookies and _____ them in her basket.
(3. bake)   (4. pack)

Then she _____ through the forest to her grandmother's house.
(5. walk)

She _____ and _____ some flowers on the way.
(6. stop)   (7. pick)

Suddenly a big bad wolf _____ out of the bushes. The wolf
(8. jump)

_____ her. He _____ her, "Little girl, where are you going?"
(9. follow)   (10. ask)

"I'm going to visit my sick grandmother," she _____ , "and I'm taking
(11. answer)

her some cookies." The wolf was happy. He _____ cookies and little girls.
(12. like)

Finally, Little Red Riding Hood _____ at her grandmother's house. She
(13. arrive)

_____ that the door was open. She _____ the house. Her
(14. notice)   (15. enter)

grandmother wasn't there. The wolf was there. When she saw the wolf, Little Red

Riding Hood took a gun out of her basket and shot him.

The wolf didn't kill her.

SIMPLE FORM VS. PAST FORM

SIMPLE PAST

GrammarGuide
4.2
6.4
4.14

She | walked | in.

She didn't | expect | to | see | the wolf.

Note: Use the simple form of the verb after *didn't* and *to*.

 Practice

Fill in the blanks with the simple form or the past form of the verb.

1. (live) Little Red Riding Hood didn't _____live_____ alone.

2. (live) She _____ with her parents.

3. (live) She didn't _____ in a big house.

4. (visit) One day she decided to _____ her grandmother.

5. (live) Her grandmother didn't _____ far away.

6. (walk) She _____ to her grandmother's house.

7. (jump) Suddenly a wolf _____ out of the bushes.

8. (follow) He _____ Little Red Riding Hood.

9. (stop) Little Red Riding Hood didn't _____ .

10. (talk) She didn't want to _____ to the wolf.

11. (want) But the wolf _____ to ask her some questions.

12. (trick) He tried to _____ her.

13. (like) She didn't _____ the wolf.

14. (like) The wolf _____ her.

15. (knock) When Little Red Riding Hood arrived at her grandmother's house, she didn't _____ on the door.

16. (walk) She _____ right in.

17. (see) She didn't expect to _____ the wolf.

18. (expect) She _____ to see her grandmother.

19. (kill) The wolf didn't _____ her.

20. (kill) She _____ the wolf.

30

The movie was boring.

ADJECTIVES ENDING IN -ED AND -ING
SIMPLE PAST

GrammarGuide
7.3

The movie bored Dave.

Dave was | bored. | The movie was | boring. |

Practice

Dave and Phil went to the new movie, "The Sharks."
Fill in the blanks with the correct form of the adjective.

The movie didn't interest Dave.

1. Dave wasn't __interested__ .

2. The movie wasn't _____ .

The sharks frightened Dave.

3. The sharks were _____ .

4. Dave was _____ .

The plot confused Dave.

5. The plot was _____ .

6. Dave was _____ .

The violence shocked Dave.

7. Dave was _____ .

8. The violence was _____ .

On the other hand, the movie entertained Phil.

9. Phil was _____ .

10. The movie was _____ .

The plot fascinated Phil.

11. The plot was _____ .

12. Phil was _____ .

The ending surprised Phil.

13. Phil was _____ .

14. The ending was _____ .

Make It Work

Fill in the dialogue. Use adjectives from the PRACTICE above.

Phil: Wasn't "The Sharks" an _____ movie?

Dave: I didn't think so. I thought the movie was _____ .

Phil: Weren't you _____ by the ending?

Dave: No. I was _____ .

New Words:

plot—story
violence—rough physical force

She attended high school for four years.

APPLICATION FOR EMPLOYMENT

Name *Linda Lee*

Address *49 Laguna Street*
Laguna Beach, California

Telephone Number *984-6621*

EDUCATION

Name of School	Major Subject	Dates Attended	Grades Completed	Degree Received
Huntington Elementary School	—	1950–1958	1st – 8th	—
Newport High School	—	1959–1963	9th – 12th	diploma
the University of California	English	1964–1968	—	bachelor's degree

Note: In the United States, students attend elementary school and junior high school for eight years. Then they attend high school for four years. When they graduate, they receive a diploma. Some students go to college or university. If they go to college for four years and graduate, they receive a bachelor's degree.

1959–1963 = from 1959 to 1963

She attended high school for four years.

AFFIRMATIVE STATEMENTS
REGULAR AND IRREGULAR PAST TENSE VERBS

GrammarGuide
4.14
6.2

When did she attend high school?

She ☐ attended ☐ high school from 1959 to 1963.

What high school did she go to?

She ☐ went ☐ to Newport High School.

 Practice

Look at the application on page 32. Then answer the questions in complete sentences.

1. What elementary school did Linda Lee go to?

   She went to Huntington Elementary School.

2. When did she attend Huntington Elementary School?

3. How long did she attend Huntington Elementary School?

4. What was the last grade she completed?

5. How long did she attend high school?

6. What high school did she go to?

7. When did she attend Newport High School?

8. What was the last grade she completed?

9. What degree did she receive?

10. What high school did she graduate from?

11. What college did she go to?

12. What was her major subject?

13. When did she attend the University of California?

14. What degree did she receive?

15. What college did she graduate from?

New Words:

**major subject–the chief course of study (history, English, math) a person takes when
completing a degree**
grade–a particular year of a school course (second grade, tenth grade)

33

He taught English at Greenfield High School.

APPLICATION FOR EMPLOYMENT

Name _Harry Smith_

Address _4224 Maple Ave_

Oakland, California

Telephone Number _921-1660_

WORK EXPERIENCE (most recent listed first)

Name of Company	Position	Work you did	Dates Worked	Yearly Salary	Reason for Leaving
Greenfield High School	English teacher	Taught English	1971-1982	$14,500	Got a job in California
Ames Dept. Store Ames, Iowa	Sales Clerk	Sold furniture	1968-1970	$7000	Got a job teaching in Massachusetts

Note: Irregular Past Tense Verbs:

teach–taught
leave–left
get–got
sell–sold

He taught English at Greenfield High School.

AFFIRMATIVE STATEMENTS
REGULAR AND IRREGULAR PAST TENSE VERBS

GrammarGuide
4.14
6.2

How long did he	work	for Ames Department Store?
He	worked	for Ames Department Store for two years.
What did he	do	at Ames Department Store?
He	sold	furniture.

Practice

Look at the application on page 34. Then answer the questions in complete sentences.

1. Where did Harry Smith work from 1971 to 1982?

   He worked at Greenfield High School.

2. What was his position?

3. What did he do?

4. How long did he work for Greenfield High School?

5. How much did he earn?

6. Why did he leave Greenfield High School?

7. Where did he work from 1968 to 1970?

8. What was his position?

9. What did he do?

10. When did he work for Ames Department Store?

11. How much did he earn?

12. Why did he leave Ames Department Store?

Make It Work

Answer the questions about your first job.

Where did you work?

What did you do?

When did you work there?

How much did you earn?

35

Why did you leave Ames Department Store?

QUESTIONS WITH *WHEN, HOW, WHY, WHAT,* AND *WHO*
REGULAR AND IRREGULAR PAST TENSE VERBS

GrammarGuide
3.7

	I left Ames Department Store.
Why	did you leave Ames Department Store?
	She graduated from high school.
What high school	did she graduate from?

Practice

Make questions.

I worked for Star Shoe Company.

1. When did you work for Star Shoe Company?

2. How long _____

She left A.B.C. Company.

3. When _____

4. Why _____

I was a secretary.

5. When _____

I earned a lot of money at Selby Company.

6. How much _____

She worked for a bank.

7. How long _____

8. Who _____ for?

I went to Harbor High School.

9. When _____

10. How long _____

He graduated from college.

11. When _____

12. What college _____ from?

Make It Work

Fill in the dialogue.

- ■ What's your sales experience?
- ☐ I worked for four years.
- ■ What _____ ?
- ☐ I sold books.
- ■ What company _____ for?
- ☐ I worked for A.B.C. Company.

36

Maloney and another man caught the thief.

AFFIRMATIVE STATEMENTS

REGULAR AND IRREGULAR PAST TENSE VERBS

GrammarGuide
4.14
6.2

have–had	come–came	catch–caught
begin–began	hear–heard	hit–hit
run–ran	find–found	
see–saw		

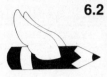

Practice

There are many stories about people who call for help and nobody comes. Here's a story about a person who called for help and everybody came.

Fill in the blanks with the correct past form.

Phyllis North, age 45, _____had_____ her purse taken from her on a street in
(1. have)

Chicago. She _____ , and then she _____ to chase the
(2. scream)   (3. start)

thief.

Michael Maloney, age 24, was driving his car down the street when he

_____ a man running and a woman running after him. Maloney
(4. see)

_____ the man with his car. When the man _____ between
(5. chase)   (6. run)

two buildings, Maloney _____ one of the buildings.
(7. hit)

Several people _____ to see what the noise was. When they
(8. come)

_____ about the thief, they _____ to chase him too. Other
(9. hear)   (10. begin)

people _____ the chase along the way.
(11. join)

Finally Maloney and another man _____ the thief and
(12. catch)

_____ the purse. Several other people _____ Phyllis North
(13. find)   (14. hear)

scream, and they all _____ the police.
(15. call)

"It was beautiful," said Maloney. "At least fifty people tried to catch the thief."

New Word:

join–take part in

37

I spent a lot of money yesterday.

IRREGULAR PAST TENSE VERBS

GrammarGuide
6.2

drive–drove	cut–cut	give–gave
write–wrote	put–put	
	read–read	take–took
spend–spent		
send–sent		do–did
	buy–bought	
have–had	bring–brought	
make–made	think–thought	hang–hung

When did you last cut your finger?

I cut my finger yesterday.
two days ago
three months ago

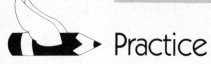

Practice

Answer the questions. Tell about yourself.

1. When did you last read a magazine?   I read a magazine two days ago.

2. When did you last give a party?

3. When did you last make an appointment?

4. When did you last have a cold?

5. When did you last drive a car?

6. When did you last write a letter?

7. When did you last take a taxi?

8. When did you last buy a book?

9. When did you last think about your family?

10. When did you last bring someone flowers?

11. When did you last do the dishes?

12. When did you last hang a picture on the wall?

13. When did you last send a telegram?

14. When did you last spend a lot of money?

15. When did you last put on a bathing suit?

She made some mistakes.

GrammarGuide
6.8

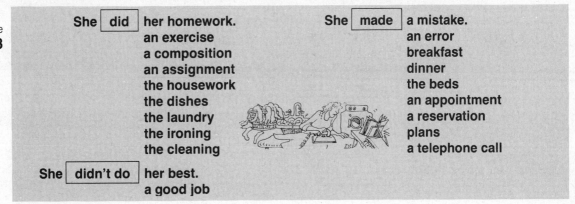

She	did	her homework.	She	made	a mistake.
		an exercise			an error
		a composition			breakfast
		an assignment			dinner
		the housework			the beds
		the dishes			an appointment
		the laundry			a reservation
		the ironing			plans
		the cleaning			a telephone call

She	didn't do	her best.
		a good job

Practice

Fill in the blanks with the correct form of *make* or *do*.

Bernadette got up early yesterday. It was a very busy day. First, she ___made___ (1.)

the beds. Then she _____ (2.) breakfast for her family and _____ (3.)

the dishes. After everyone was gone, she _____ (4.) some housework. She

washed the kitchen floor, and she dusted. She also _____ (5.) the laundry, and

then she _____ (6.) some ironing.

After lunch, she _____ (7.) a telephone call. She called her French tutor.

She _____ (8.) an appointment for 4:00 instead of 3:00. Then she quickly

_____ (9.) her homework. She had to _____ (10.) five exercises. She

_____ (11.) her best to finish, but she only _____ (12.) four exercises.

She knew that she didn't _____ (13.) a good job. She knew that she

_____ (14.) some mistakes because she _____ (15.) her homework

in a hurry. Then she got into her car and drove to her tutor's house.

New Word: tutor—private teacher

39

She gave her father a book.

INDIRECT OBJECTS
REGULAR AND IRREGULAR PAST TENSE VERBS

GrammarGuide
9.4

	Objects	
	Indirect	Direct
She served		turkey.
She served	her family	turkey.

Note: Place the indirect object before the direct object.

Practice

Add the indirect objects to the sentences.

1. Barbara Ann sent holiday cards. (her friends)

   Barbara Ann sent her friends holiday cards.

2. She mailed a gift. (her grandmother)

3. She bought gifts. (her family)

4. She got toys. (her children)

5. She gave a book. (her father)

6. She ordered flowers. (her mother)

7. She made an apron. (her sister)

8. She baked some cookies. (her aunt and uncle)

9. She got a tie. (her husband)

10. She cooked a big meal. (her family)

11. She served turkey. (everyone)

12. She read a story. (her children)

Make It Work

Tell who you gave gifts to last holiday season and tell what you gave each person.

I gave my father a scarf.

40

The waiter handed menus to them.

INDIRECT OBJECTS
REGULAR AND IRREGULAR PAST TENSE VERBS

	Objects		
	Indirect	**Direct**	**Indirect**
The waiter handed	them	menus.	
The waiter handed		menus	to them.

Note: You can place the indirect object after the direct object if you use *to* or *for* before the indirect object.

Use *to* after these verbs:
   bring give serve hand
Use *for* after these verbs:
   find pour order leave get

Practice

Rewrite the sentences, placing the indirect object after the direct object.

1. The hostess finally found them a table.   The hostess finally found a table for them.

2. The wine steward brought them some wine.

3. He poured Mr. Green some wine.

4. After Mr. Green tasted it, he poured Mr. Bang some wine.

5. Then the waiter handed them menus.

6. Mr. Green gave the waiter their order.

7. He ordered them steak.

8. After fifteen or twenty minutes, the waiter brought them their food.

9. After dinner, the waiter served them coffee and dessert.

10. When the meal was over, the waiter handed Mr. Green the check.

11. Mr. Green gave the waiter some money.

12. He also left the waiter a tip.

New Words:

wine steward–a person who serves wine
tip–a small payment for service

He left a tip for the waiter.

INDIRECT OBJECTS: *TO* OR *FOR* VS. NO PREPOSITION
REGULAR AND IRREGULAR PAST TENSE VERBS

GrammarGuide
9.4

He left the waiter a tip.

He left   a tip | for | the waiter.

Note: Use *to* or *for* when the indirect object comes
after the direct object. Do not use *to* or *for*
when the indirect object comes first.

Practice

Fill in the blanks with *to, for,* or a line (---) for nothing.

1. The hostess finally found _____---_____ them a table.

2. The hostess finally found a table _____ them.

3. The wine steward brought _____ them some wine.

4. He poured _____ Mr. Green some wine.

5. He also poured some wine _____ Mr. Bang.

6. The waiter handed _____ Mr. Green a menu.

7. Then he handed a menu _____ Mr. Bang.

8. After Mr. Green and Mr. Bang looked at the menus, Mr. Green gave their order _____ the waiter.

9. He ordered steak _____ both of them.

10. After fifteen or twenty minutes, the waiter brought _____ them their food.

11. After dinner, the waiter served dessert _____ them.

12. Then he served _____ them coffee.

13. When the meal was over, the waiter handed the check _____ Mr. Green.

14. Mr. Green gave _____ the waiter some money.

15. Mr. Green also left a tip _____ the waiter.

Make It Work

Describe a time you had dinner at an expensive restaurant.

I went out to dinner at an expensive restaurant. First, _____

_____ . _____

_____ . When the meal was over, _____

_____ .

42

She picked a black suit out.

SEPARABLE TWO-WORD VERBS
REGULAR AND IRREGULAR PAST TENSE VERBS

GrammarGuide
6.3

She | tried on | another size.

She | tried | another size | on.

Note: When the direct object is a noun, it can come either before or after the particle.

Common particles are:
out   over   off   on   back   up   down

 Practice

Change the sentences so that the noun objects come before the particles.

1. Lois looked over the suits very carefully.

   Lois looked the suits over very carefully.

2. She picked out a black suit.

   _____

3. She took off her sweater.

   _____

4. She tried on the jacket, but it didn't fit.

   _____

5. Then she picked out a gray suit.

   _____

6. The jacket fit perfectly. She went to the dressing room and put on the skirt.

   _____

7. The skirt fit, so she hung up the suit.

   _____

8. Then she took the suit to the cash register. She made out a check for $149.29.

   _____

9. She wrote down her telephone number on the back of the check.

   _____

10. The clerk folded up the suit and put it into a box.

    _____

11. Lois picked up the box and left the store.

    _____

12. She thought, "I can always take back the suit if I change my mind."

    _____

New Words:

pick out–choose; select
try on–test (for clothing)
dressing room–small room to try on clothing
look over–examine

make out–write
hang up–place on a hanger
cash register

43

I wrote them down.

SEPARABLE TWO-WORD VERBS

REGULAR AND IRREGULAR PAST TENSE VERBS

GrammarGuide
6.3

> I looked up the new words.
>
> I looked ___ the new words up.
>
> I looked | them | up.
>
> I looked the new word up.
>
> I looked | it | up.

Note: When the direct object is a noun, it can come before
or after the particle. When the direct object is
a pronoun, it comes before the particle.

Practice

Make sentences with the past tense and a direct object pronoun.

1. Turn on the light.   I turned it on. _____
2. Put on your glasses.   _____
3. Pick up a pen.   _____
4. Look over the homework assignment.   _____
5. Write down your answers.   _____
6. Fill in the blanks.   _____
7. Look up the new words in the
   dictionary.   _____
8. Read over your paper.   _____
9. Cross out your mistakes.   _____
10. Hand in the homework.   _____

Make It Work

Fill in the blanks. You can use either negative or affirmative verbs.

I last did a homework assignment on _____.
I _____it _____before I began to write.
When I was finished, I _____it _____.
I _____it _____on time.

New Words:

look up–get information from a list or dictionary
fill in–write information in spaces
read over–read again

The children down the street were playing tennis.

AFFIRMATIVE STATEMENTS
PAST CONTINUOUS

GrammarGuide
4.15

The woman on Maple Avenue | was cleaning | the house.

The children down the street | were playing | tennis.

Note: Use *was* or *were* + verb + *ing* to form the past continuous.

Practice

There was a car accident on the corner of Fifth Street and Maple Avenue at 9:30 a.m. yesterday. No one saw the accident. Tell what each person was doing at 9:30 yesterday.

Fill in the blanks with the past continuous.

1. (talk) The man on Fifth Street and Maple Avenue _____was talking_____ on the telephone.

2. (clean) The woman on Maple Avenue _____ her house.

3. (run) The man and woman on Fifth Street _____ in the park.

4. (play) The children down the street _____ tennis.

5. (sleep) The man and his son on Maple Avenue _____ .

6. (listen) The girl on Fourth Street _____ to the radio.

7. (study) The two teen-age boys in the next block _____ at the library.

8. (watch) The baby sitter on the next corner _____ the children.

9. (take) The woman in the yellow house on Maple Avenue _____ a bath.

10. (eat) The man and woman on Fifth Street _____ breakfast.

Make It Work

Here is a description of the accident.

Fill in the blanks with verbs in the past continuous.

June 5, 19 _____

Henry Abbott hit Elsie Summers at 9:30 a.m. on the corner of Fifth

Street and Maple Avenue. No one was hurt. Henry Abbott _____

a new white Chevrolet. Elsie Summers _____ a blue Ford.

Both Mr. Abbott and Mrs. Summers _____ over the speed limit.

He was studying when the doorbell rang.

AFFIRMATIVE STATEMENTS WITH *WHEN*

PAST CONTINUOUS

GrammarGuide
4.15
8.12

He was studying from 9:00 to 10:00.

The doorbell rang at 10:00.

He | was studying | when the doorbell | rang.

Note: **Use the past tense with an action that interrupts a longer, continuing action.**

continuing action: He was studying.
interrupting action: The doorbell rang.

For irregular past tense verbs, see pages 37 and 38.
Other irregular verbs:

ring–rang   eat–ate

 Practice

Combine the sentences with *when*.

1. He read the newspaper.
   The telephone rang.

   He was reading the newspaper when the telephone rang.

2. He talked on the telephone.
   The accident happened.

3. He watched television.
   Steve came over.

4. He relaxed on the patio.
   It began to rain.

5. He took a nap.
   His alarm clock accidentally went off.

6. He cooked dinner.
   The baby started to cry.

7. He ate dinner.
   He heard a loud noise.

8. He studied.
   The doorbell rang.

9. He took a bath.
   Mary called.

10. He read a book.
    The dog started to bark.

46

She hurt her back while she was moving furniture.

AFFIRMATIVE STATEMENTS WITH *WHILE*

PAST CONTINUOUS

GrammarGuide
4.15
8.12

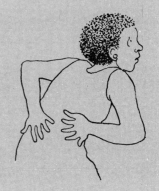

She hurt her back.
She was moving furniture.

She | hurt | her back while she | was moving | furniture.

Note: Use the past continuous with a longer, continuing action. Use the past tense with the action that interrupts the continuing action.

Irregular Past Tense Verbs:

hurt–hurt   tear–tore
cut–cut   break–broke
          fall–fell

Practice

Answer the questions with *while*.

1. When did he cut his face? (shave)

   He cut his face while he was shaving.

2. When did she hurt her back? (move furniture)

   _____

3. When did he cut his finger? (cook)

   _____

4. When did you fall down? (I/ride a bicycle)

   _____

5. When did he slip? (walk in the snow)

   _____

6. When did she bump her head? (get out of the car)

   _____

7. When did he tear his pants? (work in the yard)

   _____

8. When did you burn your hand? (I/cook)

   _____

9. When did they have an accident? (drive)

   _____

10. When did he break his leg? (play football)

    _____

He broke a glass while he was doing the dishes.

AFFIRMATIVE STATEMENTS WITH *WHEN* AND *WHILE*

PAST CONTINUOUS

GrammarGuide
4.15
8.12

While he was doing the dishes, | He broke a glass | while he was doing the dishes.
| he broke a glass. |

| He was making breakfast | when the telephone rang.
When the telephone rang, | he was making breakfast. |

Note: Use the past continuous with a longer continuing action;
use the past tense with a short, interrupting action.

 Practice

Fill in the blanks with the correct verb tense. Be sure to read each sentence first.

1. Joey <u>was sleeping</u> when his alarm clock accidently <u>went</u> off at 7:00 last Saturday
   (sleep)   (go)

   morning.

2. He _____ his face while he _____ .
        (cut)   (shave)

3. While he _____ a shower, the telephone _____ .
              (take)   (ring)

4. He _____ a shower when he _____
        (take)   (slip)

   and _____ .
         (fall)

5. The telephone _____ again while he _____ breakfast.
                    (ring)   (make)

6. While he _____ on the telephone, the toast _____
              (talk)   (begin)

   to burn.

7. He _____ the coffee when he _____ over the coffee pot.
        (make)   (knock)

8. While he _____ some eggs, he _____ his hand.
              (fry)   (burn)

9. Then he _____ a glass while he _____ the dishes.
             (break)   (do)

10. He _____ it was a bad day, so he _____ back to bed.
         (decide)   (go)

48

They've cleaned their rooms once so far.

AFFIRMATIVE STATEMENTS

PRESENT PERFECT: REGULAR PAST PARTICIPLES

GrammarGuide
4.16

She	's washed	the clothes once this week.
He	's washed	the clothes once this week.
They	've washed	the clothes once this week.
I	've washed	the clothes once this week.

Note: he's ⟶ he has
they've ⟶ they have

The present perfect is formed with *have* or *has* + the past participle. Regular past participles are formed by adding *d* or *ed* to the simple form of the verb:
change-changed   clean-cleaned

Use the present perfect for an action which began in the past and continues up to the present and possibly into the future.

 Practice

Complete the sentences with the present perfect. Use pronouns and contractions whenever possible.

1. Myra washes the clothes twice a week.

   <u>She's washed the clothes</u> once so far.

2. Roy and Becky clean up their rooms two times a week.

   _____ once so far.

3. Myra cooks dinner five nights a week.

   _____ four nights so far.

4. Roy waters the plants two or three times a week.

   _____ once so far.

5. Myra vacuums the rug twice a week.

   _____ once so far.

6. Roy and Becky clean the bathroom twice a week.

   _____ once this week.

7. Roy dusts the furniture three times a week.

   _____ twice this week.

8. Bill cooks dinner two nights a week.

   _____ once so far.

9. Myra irons the clothes twice a month.

   _____ once so far.

10. Myra and Becky change the beds four times a month.

    _____ twice so far.

New Words:

once–one time
twice–two times

49

She hasn't washed the clothes since Monday.

NEGATIVE STATEMENTS

PRESENT PERFECT: REGULAR AND IRREGULAR PAST PARTICIPLES

GrammarGuide
4.2

The last time she washed the clothes was Monday.

She | hasn't washed | the clothes since Monday.

He | hasn't | washed the clothes since Monday.

They | haven't | washed the clothes since Monday.

Note: hasn't ⟶ has not
haven't ⟶ have not

Irregular Forms:

simple form	past form	past participle
take	took	taken
feed	fed	fed
do	did	done

 Practice

Make negative sentences with *since*. Begin your sentences with a pronoun.

1. The last time Bill washed the windows was in the summer.

   He hasn't washed the windows since the summer.

2. The last time Bill took out the trash was Wednesday.

3. The last time Roy and Becky cleaned up their rooms was Tuesday.

4. The last time Becky fed the dog was yesterday.

5. The last time Myra washed the clothes was Monday.

6. The last time Myra ironed the clothes was Wednesday.

7. The last time Roy and Becky did the dishes was yesterday.

8. The last time Roy watered the plants was Tuesday.

9. The last time Bill paid the bills was last month.

10. The last time Myra vacuumed the rug was Thursday.

50

She hasn't changed the beds for two weeks.

NEGATIVE STATEMENTS WITH *SINCE* AND *FOR*
PRESENT PERFECT

GrammarGuide
4.16

She hasn't done the dishes [for] two days.

She hasn't done the dishes [since] Monday.

Note: Use *for* with a period of time; use *since* with a
beginning time.

Monday → Tuesday → Wednesday   Monday   Tuesday   Wednesday
for two days   ↑
                                           since Monday

Practice

Fill in the blanks with *for* or *since*.

1. She hasn't done the dishes _____for_____ a week.

2. She hasn't done the dishes _____since_____ Monday.

3. She hasn't vacuumed the floors _____ a month.

4. She hasn't polished the furniture _____ March.

5. She hasn't changed the beds _____ two weeks.

6. She hasn't dusted the bookshelves _____ Tuesday.

7. She hasn't washed the windows _____ May.

8. She hasn't cleaned the oven _____ two months.

9. She hasn't defrosted the refrigerator _____ last summer.

10. She hasn't waxed the kitchen floor _____ three months.

11. She hasn't watered the plants _____ a week.

12. She hasn't cleaned the bathroom _____ Saturday.

13. She hasn't taken out the trash _____ yesterday.

14. She hasn't paid the bills _____ two months.

15. She hasn't polished the silver _____ last week.

Make It Work

Fill in the blanks. Tell about yourself.

I haven't _____ for _____ .

I haven't _____ since _____ .

I haven't _____ for _____ .

Have you locked all the doors?

YES-NO QUESTIONS

PRESENT PERFECT: REGULAR AND IRREGULAR PAST PARTICIPLES

GrammarGuide
4.2

Turn down the heat.

| Have you turned | down the heat?

Note: Irregular Past Participles:
   leave–left
      take–taken
      feed–fed
   make–made

Practice

A Checklist of Things To Do Before You Leave Your House

Make questions with *you* and the present perfect tense.

1. Turn down the heat.   Have you turned down the heat?

2. Turn off the lights.   _____

3. Leave an outside light on.   _____

4. Close the windows.   _____

5. Pull down the shades.   _____

6. Take out the trash.   _____

7. Put out your cigarette.   _____

8. Make sure the oven is off.   _____

9. Feed the cat.   _____

10. Take your keys with you.   _____

11. Take your money with you.   _____

12. Lock all the doors.   _____

Make It Work

You and your friend are going out for the evening. Before you leave the house, ask your friend three important questions.

_____

_____

_____

_____

52

How many times has she fed the dog today?

QUESTIONS WITH *HOW MANY TIMES*

PRESENT PERFECT: REGULAR AND IRREGULAR PAST PARTICIPLES

GrammarGuide
3.7
6.2

Bill takes out the trash.

| How many times | has he taken out the trash?

Practice

Make questions with *how many times*.

1. Myra washes the clothes. (this week)

   How many times has she washed the clothes this week?

2. Becky feeds the dog.   (today)

   _____

3. Roy and Becky clean up their rooms. (this week)

   _____

4. Myra cooks dinner.   (this week)

   _____

5. Roy washes the car.   (this month)

   _____

6. Roy and Becky clean the bathroom. (this week)

   _____

7. Bill takes out the trash.   (this week)

   _____

8. Myra irons the clothes.   (this month)

   _____

9. Myra and Becky change the beds. (this month)

   _____

10. Roy dusts the furniture.   (this week)

   _____

Make It Work

Answer the questions in complete sentences.

How many times have you washed your hands today?

_____

How many times have you brushed your teeth today?

_____

How many times have you combed your hair today?

_____

He's already seen a travel agent.

AFFIRMATIVE STATEMENTS WITH *ALREADY*
PRESENT PERFECT: IREGULAR PAST PARTICIPLES

GrammarGuide
8.3
6.2

> He's seen a travel agent.
>
> He's [already] seen a travel agent.
>
> Note: Use *already* to show that the action was completed at the moment of speaking.
>
> Irregular Past Participles:
> | | |
> |---|---|
> | get–gotten | pay–paid |
> | see–seen | send–sent |
> | go–gone | leave–left |

 Practice

Answer the questions with the present perfect tense and *already.*

1. When is he going to go to the doctor?   He's already gone to the doctor.

2. When is he going to get a passport?   _____

3. When he is going to see a travel agent?   _____

4. When is he going to send his itinerary to his parents?   _____

5. When is he going to have his suit cleaned?   _____

6. When is he going to go to the bank?   _____

7. When is he going to buy traveler's checks?   _____

8. When is he going to get travel insurance?   _____

9. When is he going to make his hotel reservations?   _____

10. When is he going to pay for his ticket?   _____

11. When is he going to pack his suitcase?   _____

12. When is he going to leave?   _____

New Words:

itinerary–a plan of a trip, including places to be visited
traveler's checks–special checks sold by a bank to a person who is traveling
insurance–an agreement to pay money in case of an accident

54

Jack has already made his hotel reservations, but Bill hasn't made his yet.

STATEMENTS WITH *ALREADY* AND *YET*

PRESENT PERFECT

GrammarGuide
8.3

> **Jack has** | already | **made his hotel reservations,**
>
> **but Bill hasn't made his** | yet. |
>
> **Note: Use *already* in affirmative statements; use *yet* in negative statements.**

Practice

Jack and Bill are going on a business trip the day after tomorrow.
Fill in the blanks about Jack and Bill. Use *already* or *yet*.

1. Jack has ____already____ picked up his tickets, but Bill hasn't picked his up ____yet____ .

2. Bill hasn't paid for his tickets _____ , but Jack has _____ paid for his.

3. Jack hasn't gone to the bank _____ , and Bill hasn't gone to the bank _____ , either.

4. Jack has _____ seen his travel agent, but Bill hasn't seen a travel agent _____ .

5. Both Jack and Bill have _____ renewed their passports.

6. Jack has _____ made his hotel reservations, but Bill hasn't made his _____ .

7. Bill hasn't gotten travel insurance _____ , but Bill _____ has.

8. Jack has packed his suitcase _____ , but Bill hasn't started to pack his _____ .

9. Both Jack and Bill haven't had time to buy their traveler's checks _____ .

10. Bill hasn't planned his itinerary _____ , but Jack _____ has.

Make It Work

Tell two things Jack has already done.   Tell two things Jack hasn't done yet.

_____   _____

_____   _____

55

Has Jack been to France yet? Yes, he has.

NEGATIVE AND AFFIRMATIVE SHORT ANSWERS
PRESENT PERFECT

GrammarGuide
4.2

Has Jack been to France?	Yes, he has.
Have Jack and Bill been to France?	Yes, they have.
Has Jack been to Greece?	No, he hasn't.
Have Jack and Bill been to Greece?	No, they haven't.

Practice

Jack and Bill are in Europe now. They've been there for two weeks.

Jack has already visited
these countries:
   England
   France
   Germany

Bill has already visited
these countries:
   France
   Spain

Answer the questions about Jack and Bill with short answers.

1. Are Jack and Bill in Europe now?   Yes, they are.
2. Have they been there for three weeks?   No, they haven't.
3. Have they been there for two weeks? _____
4. Has Jack been to England yet? _____
5. Has Bill been to England yet? _____
6. Has Jack visited France yet? _____
7. Has Bill visited France yet? _____
8. Have Jack and Bill visited France yet? _____
9. Has Jack gone to Greece yet? _____
10. Has Bill gone to Greece yet? _____
11. Have they been to Greece yet? _____
12. Has Jack seen Spain yet? _____
13. Has Bill seen Spain yet? _____
14. Have they been to Portugal yet? _____
15. Have they been to Sweden yet? _____

Make It Work

Answer the questions. Follow the example.

Have Jack and Bill been to Germany?   Jack has, but Bill hasn't.

Have Jack and Bill visited Spain? _____

Have Jack and Bill been to England? _____

56

Do you have a car? Yes, I do.
Have you had your car for more than a month? Yes, I have.

NEGATIVE AND AFFIRMATIVE SHORT ANSWERS
SIMPLE PRESENT VS. PRESENT PERFECT

GrammarGuide
4.2

Do you have a car?	Yes, I **do.**	No, I don't.
Have you had your car for more than a month?	Yes, I **have.**	No, I haven't.

Practice

Answer the questions with negative or affirmative short answers. Answer about yourself.

1. Do you live in an apartment?

   _____ Yes, I do. OR No, I don't. _____

2. Do you live in a house?

3. Have you lived in your house or apartment for more than six months?

4. Do you own a house?
   If yes, answer this question:
   Have you owned your house for more than a year?

5. Do you work?
   If yes, answer this question:
   Have you worked at your present job for more than six months?

6. Have you ever had any large monthly payments?

7. Do you have any large debts now?

8. Have you ever had any large debts?

9. Do you have a bank account?

10. Do you have a savings account?

New Words:

own–possess; have
payment–an amount of money to be paid
debt–money owed to someone

She was a secretary from 1975 to 1977.
She's been a secretary since 1975.

Raquel Gómez
5275 High Street
Dallas, Texas
Telephone: 241-8830

RÉSUMÉ

WORK EXPERIENCE
1/77–present

Bilingual Secretary
A.B.C. Corporation
Dallas, Texas

1/75–1/77

Secretary
Selby Corporation
Houston, Texas

1/73–1/75

Receptionist
United Corporation
Santa Fe, New Mexico

1/71–1/73

Clerk Typist
Sandor, Incorporated
Carlsbad, New Mexico

Note: 1/77 = January 1977
1/20/77 = January 20, 1977

She was a secretary from 1975 to 1977.
She's been a secretary since 1975.

AFFIRMATIVE STATEMENTS

SIMPLE PRESENT, SIMPLE PAST, PRESENT PERFECT

GrammarGuide
4.17
4.4

She	's	a bilingual secretary.
She	was	a secretary from 1975 to 1977.
She	's been	a secretary since 1975.

Note: Use the past tense for actions that are finished.
Use the present perfect tense for actions that
are not finished.

 Practice

Look at the résumé on page 58. Then fill in the blanks with the correct verb tense. Use contractions whenever possible.

1. (be) She <u>'s</u> a bilingual secretary at the present time.

2. (be) She <u>was</u> a secretary from 1975 to 1977.

3. (be) She <u>'s been</u> a secretary since 1975.

4. (be) She _____ a bilingual secretary since 1977.

5. (work) She _____ in Dallas at the present time.

6. (work) She _____ for A.B.C. Corporation.

7. (start) She _____ her job at A.B.C. Corporation in 1977.

8. (work) She _____ for A.B.C. Corporation since 1977.

9. (work) From 1975 to 1977, she _____ in Houston.

10. (work) She _____ for Selby Company.

11. (live) She _____ in Houston for two years.

12. (live) She _____ in Dallas at the present time.

13. (live) She _____ in Dallas since 1977.

14. (live) She _____ in Texas since 1975.

15. (work) From 1973 to 1975, she _____ as a receptionist.

16. (work) She _____ for United Corporation from 1973 to 1975.

17. (live) She _____ in Santa Fe at that time.

18. (be) Before that, she _____ a clerk typist.

19. (live) She _____ in Carlsbad in 1972.

20. (work) She _____ for Sandor, Incorporated at that time.

The gray cat isn't as friendly as the black cat.

AS + ADJECTIVE + AS

VERB *TO BE*

GrammarGuide
7.6

The gray cat is | as healthy as | the black cat.
as old as
The gray cat isn't | as big as | the black cat.

Note: Use *as . . . as* with one, two, or three syllable adjectives. The verb can be either negative or affirmative.

THE GRAY CAT		THE BLACK CAT	
one year old	graceful	one year old	graceful
14 inches tall	friendly	16 inches tall	very friendly
9 pounds	playful	12 pounds	very playful
17 inches long	clean	17 inches long	clean
gentle	healthy	gentle	very healthy
beautiful	active	very beautiful	active

 Practice

Make sentences about the gray cat. Use *as . . . as*.

1. old — The gray cat is as old as the black cat.

2. healthy — The gray cat isn't as healthy as the black cat.

3. clean —

4. tall —

5. playful —

6. long —

7. graceful —

8. gentle —

9. friendly —

10. heavy —

11. active —

12. beautiful —

60

The apartment in Queens is cheaper.

ADJECTIVE COMPARATIVES WITH -ER AND MORE
VERB TO BE, SIMPLE PRESENT

GrammarGuide
7.5

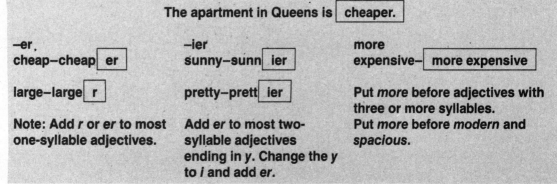

The apartment in Queens is | cheaper. |

–er,
cheap–cheap| er |

large–large| r |

Note: Add *r* or *er* to most one-syllable adjectives.

–ier
sunny–sunn| ier |

pretty–prett| ier |

Add *er* to most two-syllable adjectives ending in *y*. Change the *y* to *i* and add *er*.

more
expensive– | more expensive |

Put *more* before adjectives with three or more syllables.
Put *more* before *modern* and *spacious*.

 Practice

There are two apartments for rent. One is in Brooklyn; the other is in Queens. Compare the apartments.

Fill in the blanks with the correct comparative form.

1. (large) The apartment in Brooklyn is _____larger_____ than the apartment in Queens.

2. (modern) The kitchen is newer and is _____ .

3. (sunny) It's on the top floor, so it's _____ than the apartment in Queens.

4. (noisy) It's on a _____ street than the apartment in Queens.

5. (close) It's also _____ to transportation.

6. (small) It has a balcony, but the balcony is _____ than the balcony in the apartment in Queens.

7. (expensive) The apartment in Brooklyn is _____ than the apartment in Queens.

8. (small) The apartment in Queens is _____ than the apartment in Brooklyn.

9. (beautiful) However it's _____ .

10. (large) The living room is _____ than the living room in the apartment in Brooklyn.

11. (spacious) It's _____ , too.

12. (pretty) The apartment is on a _____ street.

New Word:

sunny—having bright sunlight

61

Bruce types faster than Carole.

Carole
types 30 words per minute
takes shorthand 90 words per minute
answers the telephone very politely
takes messages very carefully
spells accurately
gets to work very early
stays at work late
works very hard
finishes her work quickly
follows directions very carefully
dresses very neatly
gets along with people easily

Bruce
types 50 words per minute
takes shorthand 110 words per minute
answers the telephone politely
takes messages carefully
spells very accurately
gets to work early
stays at work very late
works hard
finishes his work very quickly
follows directions carefully
dresses neatly
gets along with people very easily

Bruce types faster than Carole.

ADVERB COMPARATIVES WITH *-ER* AND *MORE*

SIMPLE PRESENT

GrammarGuide
8.8

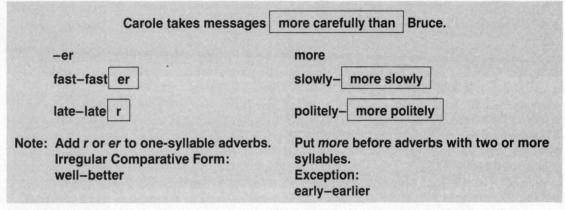

Carole takes messages | more carefully than | Bruce.

−er

fast−fast| er |

late−late| r |

Note: Add *r* or *er* to one-syllable adverbs.
Irregular Comparative Form:
well−better

more

slowly−| more slowly |

politely−| more politely |

Put *more* before adverbs with two or more syllables.
Exception:
early−earlier

Practice

Look at page 62. Then compare Carole's qualities as a secretary with Bruce's qualities.

1. Bruce types _____faster than Carole_____.

2. Bruce takes shorthand _____

3. Carole answers the telephone _____

4. Carole takes messages _____

5. Bruce spells _____

6. Carole gets to work _____

7. Bruce stays at work _____

8. Carole works _____

9. Bruce finishes his work _____

10. Carole follows directions _____

11. Carole dresses _____

12. Bruce gets along with people _____

Make It Work

Both Carole and Bruce want a raise. Tell which person deserves a raise.

_____ deserves a raise because _____ .

_____ . _____

_____

New Words:

shorthand−rapid writing where short forms are used for words and phrases
raise−an increase in salary

63

Drink less alcohol.

NOUN COMPARISONS WITH *MORE, LESS,* AND *FEWER*
IMPERATIVES

GrammarGuide
2.21

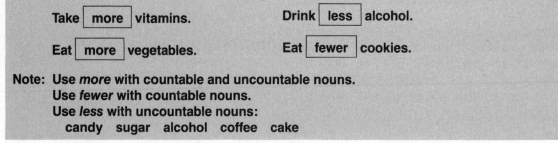

Take | more | vitamins.

Eat | more | vegetables.

Drink | less | alcohol.

Eat | fewer | cookies.

Note: Use *more* with countable and uncountable nouns.
Use *fewer* with countable nouns.
Use *less* with uncountable nouns:
   candy   sugar   alcohol   coffee   cake

 Practice

Tell someone how to stay healthy. Make sentences with *more, less,* and *fewer.*

1. vitamins   Take more vitamins.

2. cigarettes   Smoke fewer cigarettes.

3. yogurt   _____

4. candy   _____

5. sugar   _____

6. carrots   _____

7. alcohol   _____

8. eggs   _____

9. potato chips   _____

10. milk   _____

11. coffee   _____

12. cookies   _____

13. apples   _____

14. soft drinks   _____

15. cake   _____

 Make It Work

Tell other ways to stay healthy.

Get more rest.

_____

_____

_____

Alberta makes more money than Olga does.

CONTRAST: COMPARISONS WITH ADJECTIVES, ADVERBS, AND NOUNS
VERB *TO BE*, SIMPLE PRESENT

GrammarGuide
7.6
8.8
2.21

Alberta earns	more money	than Olga	does.
Alberta is	nicer	than Olga	is.
Alberta plays tennis	better	than Olga.	

 Practice

Fill in the blanks with the correct comparative form and the correct auxiliary verb or no auxiliary.

1. Alberta is 115 pounds, and Olga is 105 pounds.

    Alberta is __heavier__ __than__ Olga __is__ .

2.. Alberta is 5 feet 2 inches tall. Olga is 5 feet 4 inches tall.

    Alberta is _____ _____ Olga _____ .

3. Alberta is 30 years old. Olga is 27 years old.

    Alberta is _____ _____ Olga.

4. Alberta dresses neatly, but Olga doesn't always dress neatly.

    Alberta dresses _____ _____ _____ Olga _____ .

5. Alberta is very friendly. Olga is friendly.

    Alberta is _____ _____ _____ Olga _____ .

6. Alberta is nice, but Olga isn't always nice.

    Alberta is _____ _____ Olga _____ .

7. Alberta gets along with people very easily. Olga gets along with people easily.

    Alberta gets along with people _____ _____ _____ Olga.

8. Alberta plays tennis very well. Olga plays tennis well.

    Alberta plays tennis _____ _____ Olga _____ .

9. Alberta is very intelligent. Olga is intelligent.

    Alberta is _____ _____ _____ Olga _____ .

10. Alberta reads a lot of books. Olga reads only a few books.

    Alberta reads _____ _____ _____ Olga _____ .

65

My umbrella is different from yours.

THE SAME AS AND DIFFERENT FROM

VERB TO BE

GrammarGuide
2.21

My car is a green Ford.
Your car is a green Ford.   My car is | the same as | yours.

My car is a Ford.
Your car is a Volkswagen.   My car is | different from | yours.

Practice

Make sentences with *the same as* or *different from*.

1. My sweater is wool.
   Your sweater is nylon.

   My sweater is different from yours.

2. My gloves are brown leather.
   Your gloves are brown leather.

3. My camera is a Kodak Instamatic.®
   Your camera is a Kodak Instamatic.®

4. My umbrella is red.
   Your umbrella is black.

5. My ring is gold.
   Your ring is silver.

6. My watch is a Timex.®
   Your watch is a Timex.®

7. My slacks are gray wool.
   Your slacks are gray wool.

8. My scarf is cotton.
   Your scarf is silk.

9. My coat is navy blue wool.
   Your coat is navy blue wool.

10. My shirt is silk.
    Your shirt is polyester.

11. My wallet is brown leather.
    Your wallet is black leather.

12. My pen is a red ballpoint.
    Your pen is a red ballpoint.

Make It Work

Look at the picture. Then, compare what they're wearing.

Her shirt is the same as his.

66

Joe's Restaurant is the cheapest.

ADJECTIVE SUPERLATIVES WITH –*EST* AND *THE MOST*
VERB *TO BE*, SIMPLE PRESENT

GrammarGuide
7.5

–est cheap–cheap | est |	–iest friendly–friendl | iest |	most expensive– | most expensive |
Note: Add *est* to most one-syllable adjectives. **Irregular Superlative Form: good–best**	**Add *est* to most two-syllable adjectives ending in *y*. Change the *y* to *i* and add *est*.**	**Put *most* before adjectives with three or more syllables.** **Put *most* before two-syllable adjectives ending in *ed*: most crowded.**

Practice

Tell about these restaurants: Gerard's, Mother's, and Joe's. Fill in the blanks with the correct superlative form.

1. (fancy) Gerard's is _____the fanciest_____ restaurant of the three.

2. (elegant) It's also _____ .

3. (expensive) Gerard's, of course, is _____ restaurant of the three.

4. (slow) The service there is very slow. In fact, it has _____ service of the three.

5. (good) On the other hand, Mother's has _____ food of the three restaurants.

6. (delicious) Mother's is famous for its desserts, and it has _____ desserts.

7. (crowded) However, Mother's is usually crowded. It's _____ of the three.

8. (fast) If you want a quick, simple meal, Joe's is the place to go. It has _____ service.

9. (friendly) Joe's has _____ waitresses.

10. (cheap) It's also _____ of the three.

Make It Work

Answer the question.

Which restaurant would you eat at?

I would eat at __ _____ because it _____

and it _____ .

67

Barbara works the hardest.

Barbara

works very hard
gets to work very early
stays at work late
lives far from the office
works very carefully
works quickly
works very well under pressure
gets along with people very
easily

Mark

works hard
gets to work on time
stays at work very late
lives close to the office
works carefully
works quickly
works well under pressure
gets along with people easily

Bill

works hard
gets to work late
stays at work late
lives very far from the office
works carefully
works very quickly
works well under pressure
gets along with people easily

Barbara works the hardest.

ADVERB SUPERLATIVES WITH -*EST* AND *THE MOST*
SIMPLE PRESENT

GrammarGuide
8.8

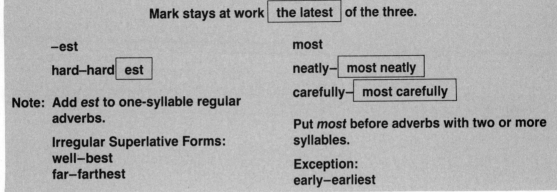

Mark stays at work ⟨ the latest ⟩ of the three.

–est	**most**
hard–hard⟨ est ⟩	neatly–⟨ most neatly ⟩
	carefully–⟨ most carefully ⟩
Note: Add *est* to one-syllable regular adverbs.	Put *most* before adverbs with two or more syllables.
Irregular Superlative Forms: well–best far–farthest	**Exception:** early–earliest

Practice

Look at page 68. Then tell about Barbara's, Mark's, and Bill's qualities as employees.
Fill in the blanks.

1. Barbara works ____the hardest____ of the three.

2. Barbara gets to work _____ .

3. Bill gets to work _____ .

4. Mark stays at work _____ .

5. Mark lives _____ to the office.

6. Bill lives _____ from the office.

7. Barbara works _____ of the three.

8. Bill works _____ .

9. Barbara works _____ under pressure.

10. Barbara gets along with people _____ .

Make It Work

All three employees want a promotion. The boss doesn't want to promote Barbara because she's a woman. Tell the boss why Barbara deserves a promotion.

Barbara is the best employee of the three. _____

_____

_____

New Words:
under pressure–in a situation where something has to be done in a hurry
promotion–an advancement in position

69

A monkey is the most intelligent.

CONTRAST: ADJECTIVE COMPARATIVES AND SUPERLATIVES

GrammarGuide
7.5
7.6

A turtle is | slower than | an ant.

A snail is | the slowest | of the three.

Note: When you are comparing two things, add *er* to adjectives or put *more* before adjectives. When you are comparing three or more things, add *est* to adjectives or put *the most* before adjectives.

Practice

Make comparative and superlative sentences about the following animals.

1. intelligent: a dog
   a horse
   a monkey

   A dog is more intelligent than a horse, but a monkey is the most intelligent of the three.

2. big: a cat
   a mouse
   a horse

3. small: a cat
   a dog
   a mouse

4. dangerous: a wasp
   a snake
   a shark

5. friendly: a cat
   a horse
   a dog

6. strong: a dog
   a cat
   a horse

7. graceful: a cat
   a dog
   a bird

8. slow: a turtle
   an ant
   a snail

9. fast: a dog
   a cat
   a horse

10. colorful: a butterfly
    a moth
    a parrot

70

The wedding will start at 3:00.

AFFIRMATIVE STATEMENTS
FUTURE WITH *WILL*

GrammarGuide
4.7

There	**will be**	champagne at the wedding.
Nick	**will drink**	champagne at the wedding.
Andrea	**will drink**	champagne at the wedding.

I	**'ll drink**	champagne at the wedding.
You	**'ll**	
He	**'ll**	
She	**'ll**	
We	**'ll**	
They	**'ll**	

Note: I'll ⟶ I will

 Practice

Fill in the blanks with the future tense. Use contractions with pronouns.

1. (have) Andrea Costas and Nick Athos __will have__ a big wedding on June fifth.

2. (be) There _____ 200 people at the wedding.

3. (start) The wedding ceremony _____ at 3:00.

4. (walk) Andrea _____ down the aisle at 3:00.

5. (wear) She _____ a long, white wedding dress.

6. (stand) She _____ beside Nick at the altar.

7. (leave) After the ceremony, Andrea and Nick _____ the church.

8. (throw) Everyone _____ rice when they leave.

9. (be) At 3:30, there _____ a wedding reception.

10. (drink) Everyone _____ champagne.

11. (cut) At 4:00, Andrea and Nick _____ the wedding cake.

12. (dance) After that, they _____ together.

13. (leave) At about 6:00, Nick and Andrea _____ the reception.

14. (get) They _____ into a car that says, "Just Married".

15. (drive) They _____ off.

New Words:

    aisle   **altar**

reception–a large formal party
champagne–French white wine
ceremony–a special formal set of actions for an important public or religious event

71

Andrea's sister will get the flowers.

AGREEMENT WITH *WILL*

Andrea's sister | **will get** | **the flowers.**

Note: she'll ⟶ she will
  he'll ⟶ he will

Practice

Nick Athos and Andrea Costas are getting married this summer.
It's going to be a big wedding. Everyone in both families will help.

Make sentences with *will* to show who has agreed to help.
Use contractions with pronouns.

1. They asked Andrea's sister to get the flowers.

   Andrea's sister will get the flowers.

2. They asked Nick's aunt to reserve the church.

3. They also asked her to make the wedding dress.

4. They asked Andrea's cousin to make a wedding cake.

5. They asked Andrea's parents to have the reception at their house.

6. They asked Nick's parents to give a party too.

7. They asked Andrea's brother to sing a song.

8. They also asked him to play the piano.

9. They asked Andrea's father to read a poem.

10. They asked Nick's brother to drive them to the reception.

11. They also asked him to take photos.

12. They asked Andrea's grandmother to serve the champagne.

72

When my sister gets married, she'll have a big wedding.

AFFIRMATIVE STATEMENTS WITH *AFTER*, *BEFORE*, AND *WHEN*

FUTURE WITH *WILL*

GrammarGuide
4.7
8.12

When my sister | gets | married next month, she | 'll have | a big wedding.

My sister will have a big wedding when she gets married next month.

Note: To express a future idea, use the present tense in clauses beginning with *when, after,* or *before.* Use the future tense in the main clause.

Practice

Read each sentence first. Then fill in the blanks with the correct verb tense.

1. When my sister _____gets_____ married next month, she and her husband
   (get)
   _____will have_____ a big wedding.
   (have)

2. Diane _____ beautiful when she _____ down the aisle.
   (look)   (walk)

3. After the ceremony, _____ over, she and her husband
   (be)
   _____ the church.
   (leave)

4. A photographer _____ their picture before they _____
   (take)   (leave)
   the church.

5. When they _____ the church, everyone _____ rice.
   (leave)   (throw)

6. After Diane and her husband _____ at the reception, everyone
   (arrive)
   _____ champagne.
   (drink)

7. After Diane and her husband _____ , everyone _____ .
   (dance)   (dance)

8. Diane _____ a bouquet of flowers before she and her husband
   (throw)
   _____ the reception.
   (leave)

9. The person who catches it _____ the next person to get married.
   (be)

10. After Diane _____ the bouquet, she and her husband
    (throw)
    _____ into a car and drive away.
    (get)

73

After Yukiko leaves Tokyo, she'll go to London.

AFFIRMATIVE STATEMENTS WITH *AFTER* AND *WHEN*

FUTURE WITH *WILL*

GrammarGuide
4.7
8.12

> **Yukiko will leave Tokyo.**
> **She'll go to London.**
>
> After Yukiko │ leaves │ Tokyo, she │ 'll go │ to London.
>
> Note: **Use the present tense in clauses beginning with
> *when* or *after*. Use the future tense in the main clause.**
>
> **Put a comma after the *when* or *after* clause if
> it comes first in the sentence.**

 Practice

Combine the sentences with *after* or *when*.

1. First, Yukiko will leave Tokyo.
   Then, she'll go to London.

   After Yukiko leaves Tokyo, she'll go to London.

2. She'll see London.
   After that, she'll fly to Paris.

   After _____

3. She'll be in Paris.
   At that time, she'll see the
   Cathedral of Notre Dame.

   When _____

4. She'll leave Paris.
   Then she'll go to Rome.

   After _____

5. She'll visit Rome.
   She'll go to some museums.

   When _____

6. She'll be in Rome.
   She'll see a lot of famous fountains.

   When _____

7. She'll see Rome.
   Afterwards, she'll go to Madrid.

   After _____

8. She'll spend a day in Madrid.
   Then she'll go to Athens.

   After _____

9. She'll visit Athens.
   She'll see some famous statues.

   When _____

10. She'll leave Athens.
    She'll fly back to Tokyo.

    After _____

New Words:

fountain   statue

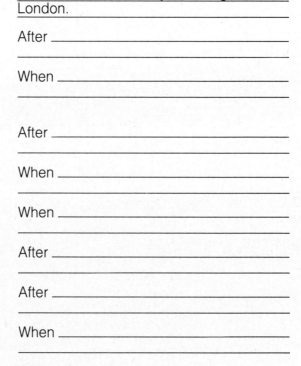

74

You will stay in a hotel on the Mediterranean.

**NO ARTICLE VS. *THE* WITH COUNTRIES,
BODIES OF WATER, AND MOUNTAINS
FUTURE WITH *WILL***

GrammarGuide
2.9

Countries and Cities	Bodies of Water	Mountains
☐ France Rome	the Rhine the Atlantic Ocean the Mediterranean Sea	the Alps the Pyrenees
the Soviet Union the United States	☐ Lake Lucerne Lake Lausanne	☐ Mt. Vesuvius Mt. Olympus

Note: Use no article with cities and countries. Use *the* with political units like the Soviet Union.

Use *the* with rivers, oceans, and seas.
Use no article with lakes and bays.

Use *the* with mountain ranges.
Use no article with the name of a single mountain.
Exception: the Matterhorn.

Practice

Fill in the blanks with *the* or a line (---) for nothing. A TOUR OF EUROPE

Day One: You will leave __the__ United States in the evening and arrive in __---__
                      (1.)   (2.)
             Europe the next day. You will fly over _____ Atlantic Ocean aboard a jet.
                                                                      (3.)

Day Two: You will arrive in _____ France.
                                        (4.)

Day Three: You will be driven by bus to _____ Germany.
                                                  (5.)

Day Four: You will take a scenic boat trip on _____ Rhine River.
                                                        (6.)

Day Five: You will be driven to _____ Switzerland. You will stay in a fabulous hotel
                                          (7.)
             on _____ Lake Lucerne.
                   (8.)

Day Six: You will be driven through _____ Alps, the most beautiful mountains in
                                              (9.)
             the world.

Day Seven: You will arrive in _____ sunny Italy.
                                   (10.)
             You will stay in a hotel on _____ Mediterranean Sea.
                                            (11.)

Day Eight: You will take a train to southern Italy. You will see _____ Mount Vesuvius.
                                                                        (12.)
             That night, you will fly back to the United States.

75

Roy won't clean up his room.

REFUSAL WITH *WON'T*

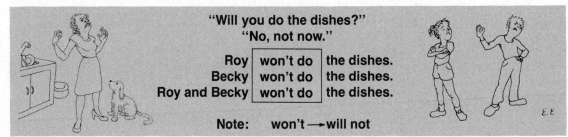

GrammarGuide
5.8

"Will you do the dishes?"
"No, not now."

Roy	won't do	the dishes.
Becky	won't do	the dishes.
Roy and Becky	won't do	the dishes.

Note: won't → will not

Practice

Read each dialogue. Then make a sentence with *won't.*

| Myra: | Will you please clean up your room? | 1. <u>Roy won't clean up his room.</u> |
| Roy: | Not now. I'm busy. | |

| Myra: | Will you please do your homework? | 2. _____ |
| Roy and Becky: | We did our homework yesterday. | _____ |

| Myra: | Would you please take out the trash? | 3. _____ |
| Roy: | Not now. I'll do it later. | _____ |

| Myra: | It's time to practice the piano. | 4. _____ |
| Becky: | I refuse. I hate to practice. | _____ |

| Myra: | Would you like to feed the dog? | 5. _____ |
| Roy: | I fed the dog yesterday. It's Becky's turn. | _____ |

| Myra: | Will you and Becky please turn off the television set? | 6. _____ |
| Roy and Becky: | No. We're watching our favorite program. | _____ |

| Myra: | Will you set the table? | 7. _____ |
| Becky: | I refuse. That's Roy's job. | _____ |

| Myra: | Please put the soda back in the refrigerator. | 8. _____ |
| Becky: | No. I didn't use it last. | _____ |

| Myra: | Please eat everything on your plate. | 9. _____ |
| Roy: | I can't. I'm too full. | _____ |

| Myra: | Will you please do the dishes? | 10. _____ |
| Roy and Becky: | We're sorry, but we have to do our homework now. | _____ |

They'll help themselves when they get hungry.

REFLEXIVE PRONOUNS

SIMPLE PRESENT, FUTURE WITH *WILL*

GrammarGuide
3.8

I'll enjoy	myself.		We'll enjoy	ourselves.
You'll enjoy	yourself.		You'll enjoy	yourselves.
He'll enjoy	himself.		They'll enjoy	themselves.
She'll enjoy	herself.			

Note: Reflexive pronouns refer back to the subject of the sentence.

Practice

Fill in the dialogue with the correct reflexive pronouns.

Baby sitter: Hi, I'm the baby sitter.

Mrs. Taylor: Hello. Please come in. Make _____yourself_____ at home.
(1.)

There's lots of food in the refrigerator. Please help _____ .
(2.)

Baby sitter: Don't worry about me. I'll fix _____ something to eat. What
do the children like to eat? (3.)

Mrs. Taylor: They'll help _____ when they get hungry.
(4.)

Baby sitter: Fine.

Mrs. Taylor: I don't want Greg to climb any trees. He sometimes falls and hurts

_____ . And watch Melissa. Yesterday she burned
(5.)

_____ on the stove.
(6.)

Baby sitter: Don't worry. I'll watch her. What do the children like to do?

Mrs. Taylor: Oh, they'll amuse _____ . My husband and I will be at the
(7.)

Peterson's house. The number is 283-3306. Call us if the children don't

behave _____ .
(8.)

Baby sitter: I will. I hope you and Mr. Taylor enjoy _____.
(9.)

Mrs. Taylor: Thank you. I'm sure we'll enjoy _____.
(10.)

New Words:

amuse–spend time in a pleasant way   **behave–act in a proper manner**

I'd take a knife with me on the lifeboat.

NEGATIVE AND AFFIRMATIVE STATEMENTS
PRESENT UNREAL CONDITIONAL

GrammarGuide
5.9
5.2

If you were shipwrecked, what would you take with you on the lifeboat?

I | 'd take | a knife with me.

I | wouldn't take | any money.

Note: **I'd** ⟶ **I would**
wouldn't ⟶ **would not**

Practice

Tell which six things you would take with you on the lifeboat and which six things you wouldn't take.

1. some money   I wouldn't take any money.
2. some matches
3. a pen
4. some paper
5. an umbrella
6. a knife
7. a candy bar
8. a blanket
9. a can opener
10. a flashlight
11. a radio
12. some cigarettes
13. a book

Make It Work

If you were allowed to take only two things on the lifeboat, which things would they be?

78

If I were a corporation president, I'd make a lot of money.

AFFIRMATIVE STATEMENTS WITH *WERE*
PRESENT UNREAL CONDITIONAL

GrammarGuide
4.23
8.14

If I [**were**] a movie star, I [**'d be**] in the movies.

Note: Use *if* + *were* and *would* + simple form of the verb for unreal possibilities in the present. Use *were* for all persons.

I'd → I would

When the sentence begins with *if*, put a comma after the *if* clause.

Practice

First answer each question with *yes* or *no.* Then make sentences for every question you answered with *no.*

1. Are you a movie star?

   No. If I were a movie star, I'd make a cowboy movie.

2. Are you an artist?

3. Are you a doctor?

4. Are you a corporation president?

5. Are you a pilot?

6. Are you a photographer?

7. Are you a secretary?

8. Are you a pianist?

9. Are you a novelist?

10. Are you a gardener?

Make It Work

What would you do if you were the leader of your country?

If _____ , _____ .

I _____ .

79

If someone stole my wallet, I'd call the police.

AFFIRMATIVE STATEMENTS
PRESENT UNREAL CONDITIONAL

GrammarGuide
4.23
8.14

> If I [saw] a car accident, I ['d call] an ambulance.
>
> If the car [were] on fire, I ['d call] the fire department.
>
> **Note: Use the past tense with *if* clauses.**
>   **Irregular Past Tense Verbs:**
>   **lose–lost**   **break–broke**
>   **feel–felt**   **steal–stole**

Practice

Answer the questions in complete sentences.

1. Who would you call if you had a personal problem?

   If I had a personal problem, I'd call my mother.

2. Who would you call if you needed money?

3. What would you do if you had a headache?

4. What would you do if you felt sick?

5. Who would you call if you broke your arm?

6. Who would you call if your house were on fire?

7. Who would you call if you saw a car accident?

8. Who would you call if someone robbed your house or apartment?

9. What would you do if you lost the keys to your apartment?

10. Who would you call if someone stole your wallet?

Make It Work

Fill in the blanks with emergency telephone numbers in your area.

ambulance _____
police department _____
fire department _____

80

You should pay attention to sales.

SHOULD AND SHOULDN'T

GrammarGuide
5.14
5.2

You	should	make	a shopping list.
You	shouldn't	shop	on an empty stomach.

Note: shouldn't ⟶ should not
Use *should* for advice or suggestions.

Practice

Give advice to someone who wants to save money on food. Use *should* or *shouldn't*.

1. Pay attention to sales. —— You should pay attention to sales.

2. Don't buy food you can't use. —— You shouldn't buy food you can't use.

3. Plan your meals in advance. ——

4. Use coupons. ——

5. Don't buy fresh fruit and vegetables out of season. ——

6. Compare prices of several brands. ——

7. Buy store brands. ——

8. Buy large boxes and cans. ——

9. Don't buy a lot of processed food. ——

10. Don't buy more fresh food than you need. ——

11. Keep food carefully. ——

12. Don't buy food you don't want just because it's on sale. ——

13. Check the expiration date on dairy products. ——

14. Buy frozen food last. ——

15. Don't shop on an empty stomach. ——

New Words:

expiration date–the last date food can be sold
brand–a group of products made by a certain company
processed food–food that is preserved (canned food,
    frozen food, food in boxes)

coupon

81

She'd better not walk home alone.

HAD BETTER AND HAD BETTER NOT

GrammarGuide
5.15

It's very late at night, and Mary wants to walk home alone.

| She | 'd better not walk | home alone. |
| She | 'd better take | a taxi. |

Note: she'd better ⟶ she had better
she'd better not ⟶ she had better not

Use *had better* to express advice in particular situations.

Practice

Read each situation. Then give advice, first with *had better not* and then with *had better*. Use contractions.

It's very late at night. A group of Mary's friends offer to walk home with her, but she wants to walk home alone.

1. She'd better not walk home alone.

2. She'd better walk with her friends.

A friend has bought some shoes in a department store. He takes out his wallet to pay for the shoes and leaves his wallet on the counter.

3. _____

4. _____

A friend is leaving her house. As she walks away, she leaves the door unlocked.

5. _____

6. _____

A friend is going to walk home late at night. She refuses to take a taxi.

7. _____

8. _____

A friend parks his car on the street. He leaves his camera in the car.

9. _____

10. _____

A friend is going away on a vacation. She locks the door of her apartment, but she leaves the windows open.

11. _____

12. _____

82

You must buy your ticket in advance.

NECESSITY WITH *MUST* AND OBLIGATION WITH *HAVE TO*

GrammarGuide
5.16

You	must		fasten	your seatbelt.
You	have	to	fasten	your seatbelt.

Note: Use *must* and *have to* to express necessity and obligation. In affirmative statements, there is little difference in meaning between *must* and *have to*.

Practice

Fill in the blanks with *must* or *have to* and the verb (in parentheses).

1. (buy) You __must__ __buy__ your ticket in advance.

2. (confirm) You __have__ __to__ __confirm__ your flight ahead of time.

3. (be) You _____ _____ _____ at the airport thirty minutes ahead of time.

4. (check in) You _____ _____ at the reservation counter.

5. (reserve) You _____ _____ _____ a seat on the plane.

6. (check) You _____ _____ your suitcases.

7. (get) You _____ _____ _____ a boarding pass.

8. (go) You _____ _____ _____ through security.

9. (wait) You _____ _____ until your flight is announced.

10. (show) You _____ _____ your ticket and your boarding pass to the flight attendant.

11. (sit) You _____ _____ _____ in your reserved seat.

12. (fasten) You _____ _____ your seatbelt.

Make It Work

Name two things you have to do ahead of time if you are going on a plane trip.

_____

_____

Name three things you must do at the airport before you can get on the plane.

_____

_____

_____

New Words:

confirm–make certain of
ahead of time–in advance
reserve–keep for future use
boarding pass–a card you must have to enter an airplane
security–an area where your suitcases and bags are searched

83

You don't have to stop, but you must not speed.

DON'T HAVE TO VS. MUST NOT

GrammarGuide
5.16

You | must not drive | faster than 55 miles an hour.

You | don't have to drive | 55 miles an hour. You can

drive slower.

Note: **must not = prohibited**
don't have to = not necessary

Practice

Look at the signs. Then fill in the blanks with *don't have to* or *must not*.

1. You _____must not_____ drive faster than 25 miles an hour.

2. You _____ drive 25 miles an hour. You can drive slower.

3. You must slow down, but you _____ stop.

4. You _____ speed.

5. If a train is coming, you _____ go.

6. If there's no train coming, you _____ stop, but you should slow down.

7. You _____ turn left.

8. You _____ turn right, but you can if you want to.

9. You _____ stop.

10. You must slow down. You _____ drive faster than 25 miles an hour.

Equivalent:

mile = 1.6 kilometers

84

She must be a police officer.

ASSUMPTIONS WITH *MUST*

GrammarGuide
5.16

What is he?

He | **must be** | an accountant.

Note: Use *must* to express an assumption when you are almost sure that it's true.

Practice

Make guesses or assumptions about their occupations. Choose from the list below.

police officer	carpenter
✓cowboy	doctor
dancer	waitress
painter	business executive
boxer	musician

1. He's wearing jeans, a big hat, and boots.   He must be a cowboy.

2. He's wearing a white uniform and he's carrying a black bag.   _____

3. She's wearing a dark uniform, and she's carrying a gun.   _____

4. He has paint all over his jeans.   _____

5. He has a broken jaw and his eye is black and blue.   _____

6. She's wearing a black uniform with a white apron.   _____

7. She has a suit on, and she's carrying a briefcase.   _____

8. He's wearing a black suit and a bow tie. He's carrying a violin.   _____

9. He's wearing ballet shoes and a black leotard.   _____

10. He has overalls on, and he's carrying a hammer.   _____

New Words:

black and blue—skin that is a dark color because of an injury

He might be lost.

MIGHT AND MIGHT NOT

GrammarGuide
5.12
5.2

Where do you suppose Gary is?

He | might   be | lost.

He | might not know | how to get here.

Note: *Might not* is not contracted.

Use *might* to express possibility.
Use *must* when you are almost sure something
is true. Use *might* when you are less certain.

Practice

You are having a party. It's 10:30, and Gary isn't at the party yet. Make some guesses about why he isn't at the party. Use *might* or *might not*.

1. Perhaps he's at another party.   He might be at another party.

2. Perhaps he has something else to do tonight.

3. Perhaps he doesn't know that the party is tonight.

4. Perhaps he's sick.

5. Perhaps he doesn't know what time the party starts.

6. Perhaps he doesn't know the address.

7. Perhaps he's lost.

8. Perhaps he doesn't know how to get here.

9. Perhaps he's in a traffic jam.

10. Perhaps he's in trouble.

Make It Work

Your teacher is twenty minutes late for class.
Make sentences about your teacher.
He/she might be in a traffic jam.

She'd rather eat at a restaurant.

WOULD RATHER AND WOULD RATHER NOT

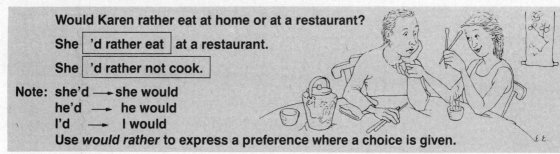

GrammarGuide
5.10

Would Karen rather eat at home or at a restaurant?

She | 'd rather eat | at a restaurant.

She | 'd rather not cook. |

Note: she'd ⟶ she would
he'd ⟶ he would
I'd ⟶ I would
Use *would rather* to express a preference where a choice is given.

 Practice

Look at the dialogue. Then fill in the blanks with *would rather* or *would rather not*. Use contractions with pronouns.

Karen: Would you rather eat at home or at a restaurant?
Charlie: I'd rather eat at home.
Karen: I'd rather not cook dinner. Let's eat out. Afterwards, let's go to a movie.
Charlie: I'd rather not. Let's watch television.
Karen: Let's compromise. We'll eat out, and then we'll go home. Would you rather eat Chinese food or Italian food?
Charlie: I'd rather eat Italian food.
Karen: I don't feel like Italian food. I'd rather eat Chinese food. Would you rather eat at Ming's Restaurant or The Great Wall?
Charlie: The Great Wall. Let's eat at Ming's.

1. Charlie <u>would rather not eat</u> at a restaurant.

2. He _____ at home.

3. Karen _____ at home.

4. She _____ dinner.

5. She _____ at a restaurant.

6. Charlie _____ Italian food.

7. Karen _____ Italian food.

8. She _____ Chinese food.

9. She _____ at Ming's.

10. Charlie _____ at The Great Wall.

11. Karen _____ television at home.

12. She _____ to a movie.

13. Charlie _____ to a movie.

14. He _____ home after dinner.

15. He _____ television.

87

I'd rather go to a fancy restaurant.

WOULD LIKE VS. WOULD RATHER

GrammarGuide
5.10

Would you like to go to The Great Wall?	**No, I wouldn't.**
Would you like to go to Ming's Restaurant?	**Yes, I would.**
Would you rather go to Ming's or The Great Wall?	**I'd rather go to Ming's.**

Note: *Would like* expresses preference when there is usually one choice.
Would rather expresses preference when there is more than one choice.

Practice

Answer the questions. Tell about yourself.

1. Would you like to eat out tonight? _____No, I wouldn't. OR Yes, I would._____

2. Would you like to have pizza? _____

3. Would you rather eat French food or Italian food? _____

4. Would you rather have pizza or steak? _____

5. Would you like to get dressed up tonight? _____

6. Would you rather go to a fancy restaurant or a casual restaurant? _____

7. Would you like to do something afterwards? _____

8. Would you rather go somewhere or stay at home? _____

9. Would you like to watch television? _____

10. Would you rather go to a movie or watch television? _____

Make It Work

You are entertaining a very important person who is spending time in your town. Ask about his or her preferences for an evening. Fill in the dialogue.

■ _____?
□ Yes, I would.
■ _____?
□ I'd rather go to a French restaurant.
■ _____?
□ I'd rather go home afterwards. I'm very tired.

88

I won't do it.

MODAL AND TENSE REVIEW

Practice

GrammarGuide
5.17 Look at the pictures. Then fill in each blank with one of the following words. Use each word one time.

am	was	can't	will	must
is	did	won't	would	✓might

1. I _____might_____ hurt myself.

2. I _____ do it.

3. I _____ do it.

4. Everyone _____ watching me.

5. I _____ do it.

6. I _____ do it.

7. I _____ doing it.

8. I _____ it.

9. That _____ fun!

10. I _____ like to do it again.

They had to clean the entire house.

HAD TO

GrammarGuide
5.16

> **The inside of the house needed paint.**
>
> They | **had to paint** | the inside of the house.
>
> **Note: Use the simple form of the verb with *had to*.**

Practice

Paul and Laura own a beautiful old house. When they bought the house a year ago, it needed a lot of work. Here are some of the things they had to do before they moved into the house.

Make sentences with *had to*.

1. The entire house was a mess. (clean)   They had to clean the entire house.

2. All the windows were dirty. (wash)   _____

3. The house had no screens. (put in)   _____

4. The stove was in bad condition. (fix)   _____

5. There wasn't a refrigerator. (buy)   _____

6. The kitchen didn't have a counter. (build)   _____

7. The inside of the house needed to be painted. (paint)   _____

8. The roof was in bad condition. (fix)   _____

9. The house didn't have an air conditioner. (buy)   _____

10. There were no light fixtures. (put in)   _____

Make It Work

When you moved into your apartment or house, what things did you have to do?

I had to clean my apartment.

_____

_____

_____

New Word:

light fixture

90

He didn't have to buy a new stove.

DIDN'T HAVE TO

GrammarGuide
5.2
5.16

> His house came with a new stove.
>
> He | didn't have to buy | a new stove when he moved in.

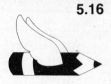

Practice

John bought a new house. When he bought his house a year ago, he moved right in.

Make negative sentences with *have to*.

1. The house came with screens. (put in)   He didn't have to put in screens.

2. It came with a refrigerator. (buy)   _____

3. It came with a new stove. (buy)   _____

4. It had a large counter in the kitchen. (build)   _____

5. The inside of the house didn't need paint. (paint)   _____

6. The roof wasn't in bad condition. (fix)   _____

7. It came with new light fixtures. (put in)   _____

8. It had new rugs. (buy)   _____

9. It had a built-in air conditioner. (put in)   _____

10. The windows were clean. (wash)   _____

Make It Work

Name three things you didn't have to do when you moved into your house or apartment.

_____

_____

_____

He could read without his glasses ten years ago.

PAST ABILITY WITH *COULD*

GrammarGuide
5.7

He can't read without his glasses.

He could read **without his glasses ten years ago.**

Note: Use *could* to express ability in the past tense.

Practice

Make sentences with *could*.

1. My father can't swim a mile.
   _____He could swim a mile_____ ten years ago.

2. My father can't play tennis all day.
   _____ ten years ago.

3. My father can't read without his glasses.
   _____ ten years ago.

4. My father can't go out every night.
   _____ ten years ago.

5. My father can't stay up all night.
   _____ ten years ago.

6. My father can't run up and down the stairs.
   _____ ten years ago.

7. My father can't lift heavy objects.
   _____ ten years ago.

8. My father can't eat rich food.
   _____ ten years ago.

9. My father can't work for twelve hours a day.
   _____ ten years ago.

10. My father can't run a mile in fifteen minutes.
    _____ ten years ago.

Make It Work

What could you do ten years ago that you can't do now?

I could stay up all night.

_____

_____

_____

_____

We couldn't go anywhere.

COULDN'T VS. HAD TO

GrammarGuide
5.7
5.16

There wasn't any public transportation.

We	couldn't		go	anywhere.
We	had	to	stay	at home.

Note: couldn't → could not

Use *couldn't* + simple form of verb; use *had* + *to* +
simple form of verb.

Remember that *could* = ability and *had to* = necessity.

Practice

Fill in the blanks with *couldn't* or *had to* and the verb in parentheses. Be sure to read the
entire sentence first.

There was a terrible snowstorm in New Jersey last winter. The town my family and I
live in had nine feet of snow. It was so cold that we _couldn't start_ our car. There
(1. start)

wasn't any public transportation, so we _____ anywhere by bus. When we
(2. go)

wanted to go somewhere, we _____ . A few grocery stores were open,
(3. walk)

but there weren't any food deliveries. We _____ any fresh food, such as
(4. buy)

milk, bread, or vegetables. We _____ canned food. The telephones were
(5. buy)

out of order, so we _____ our telephone. We _____ cold
(6. use)   (7. take)

showers because there wasn't any hot water. There wasn't any electricity, either. We

_____ the lights. We _____ candles at night. Of course, we
(8. use)   (9. use)

_____ television. Because the stove is electric, it wasn't working either.
(10. watch)

We _____ anything. We _____ cold food for two days.
(11. cook)   (12. eat)

New Words:
canned food–food in cans
out of order–not working

candle 🕯️   electricity 🔌

93

She used to live with her parents.

USED TO

GrammarGuide
5.9

I
He
She
We
You
They
| used to collect | stamps.

Note: *Used to* **expresses a recurring action in the past.**

 Practice

Make sentences with *used to*.

1. She doesn't live in a small town anymore.

She used to live in a small town.

2. She doesn't live with her parents anymore.

3. She doesn't play with dolls anymore.

4. She doesn't wear cowboy hats and blue jeans anymore.

5. She doesn't dress up in her mother's clothes anymore.

6. She doesn't climb trees anymore.

7. She doesn't play baseball in the street anymore.

8. She doesn't collect stamps anymore.

9. She doesn't take ballet lessons anymore.

10. She doesn't read comic books anymore.

 Make It Work

What used to be true about you that isn't true now?

I used to live with my parents.

94

You didn't use to like concerts.

DIDN'T USE TO

GrammarGuide
5.9

> **I like spinach.**
>
> **You** | **didn't use to like** | **spinach.**
>
> **Note: Omit the _d_ in _used to_ when you make negative statements.**

Practice

Make negative responses with _used to._ Begin your sentences with _you._

1. I like spinach.   Really? <u>You didn't use to like spinach.</u>

2. I drink coffee.   Oh? _____

3. I smoke a lot.   Really? _____

4. I like to be alone.   Oh? _____

5. I read a lot.   Oh, really? _____

6. I wear glasses.   Really? _____

7. I enjoy classical music.   No kidding! _____

8. I like concerts.   Really? _____

9. I like modern art.   Oh? _____

10. I enjoy serious discussions.   No kidding! _____

11. I like foreign films.   Really? _____

12. I like to study.   No kidding! _____

Make It Work

What's true about you now that didn't use to be true?

<u>I didn't use to be talkative.</u>

_____

_____

_____

95

"Hey, stop!" he shouted.

PUNCTUATION

DIRECT SPEECH

GrammarGuide
11.8

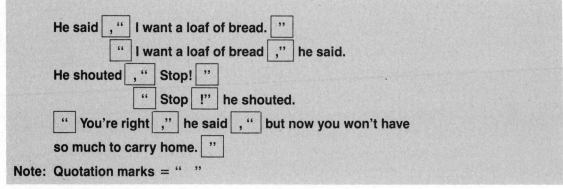

He said [,"] I want a loaf of bread. ["]

["] I want a loaf of bread [,"] he said.

He shouted [,"] Stop! ["]

["] Stop [!"] he shouted.

["] You're right [,"] he said [,"] but now you won't have

so much to carry home. ["]

Note: Quotation marks = " "

 Practice

Add the quotation marks and commas (,) to the sentences.

A boy went into a bakery and said to the clerk, "I'd like a loaf of bread, please."

The clerk gave him a loaf of bread. Then he said That'll be seventy-five cents, please.

This is a very small loaf for seventy-five cents the boy said.

Perhaps you are right the clerk said but now you won't have so much to carry home.

He laughed and held his hand out for the money.

That's true the boy replied. He gave the clerk fifty cents and went to the door.

Hey, stop! the man shouted. This isn't enough money!

Perhaps you are right the boy said but now you won't have so much to count.

New Words:

reply—answer
shout—say in a loud voice

She said, "Go to the store and get me a loaf of bread."

ARTICLES *A* VS. *THE*
DIRECT AND INDIRECT SPEECH

GrammarGuide
2.7

She said, "Open [a] can of dog food. Then feed [the] dog."

She told me to go to [the] grocery store and get her [a] loaf of bread.

"Shut [the] curtains. [The] sun is too bright," she said.

Note: Use *the* when you refer to only one of something: the moon   the sun

Use *the* for objects at home or in the community when people know which one you are talking about: the grocery store   the refrigerator

Use *a* for unspecified objects: a can of dog food

Don't use *a* with plural nouns or uncountable nouns: rain   snow   weather

Practice

Fill in the blanks with *a* or *the*.

1. She told me to go into __the__ kitchen and get her __a__ glass of water.

2. She said, "Please bring me _____ sweater. It's in _____ closet upstairs."

3. "Shut _____ curtains. _____ sun is too bright," she said.

4. She told me to go to _____ drugstore and get her _____ newspaper.

5. She said, "Open _____ can of dog food and then feed _____ dog."

6. "Go to _____ cupboard and get me _____ plate," she said to me.

7. She said, "Please answer _____ door. _____ doorbell is ringing."

8. "Come outside and look at _____ moon," she said.

9. She said, "Close _____ windows. _____ rain is coming into _____ house."

10. "Please bring me _____ cigarette. They're on _____ table," she said.

11. She said, "Look at _____ clouds in _____ sky. It's going to rain."

12. She told me to go to _____ supermarket and buy _____ quart of milk.

New Words:

cloud   moon   sky

He told the police that he was at the park all afternoon.

SAY VS. *TELL*

DIRECT AND INDIRECT SPEECH

GrammarGuide
6.5

Direct Speech

He | said, | "I can't tell you the exact time."

He | said | to the police, "I can't tell you the exact time."

Indirect Speech

He | said | that he couldn't tell them the exact time.

He | told | the police that he couldn't tell them the exact time.

Note: **Use *say* with the exact words of the speaker; use *say* or *tell* with indirect speech. Use *say* without an indirect object or with *to* + indirect object. Use *tell* with an indirect object without *to*.**

Use *tell* with the following expressions:
  tell the truth   tell a lie   tell a story   tell the time

In informal situations, the past tense is sometimes used in place of the past perfect tense in indirect speech.

98

He told the police that he was at the park all afternoon.

Practice

The police arrived at Hilda de Mendoza's house at 3:15. Mrs. de Mendoza was dead. The police questioned the servants, the lawyer, and Mrs. de Mendoza's family. This is what each person said.

Look at page 98. Then fill in the blanks with *said* or *told*.

1. The lawyer __said__ to the police, "I had an appointment with Mrs. de Mendoza at 3:00."

2. He _____ the police that Mrs. de Mendoza was planning to change her will.

3. Then the lawyer _____ , "When I walked into the study, I found her lying on the floor."

4. The butler _____ the police that Mrs. de Mendoza's lawyer arrived exactly at 3:00.

5. Hector de Mendoza _____ the police that he was at the park all afternoon.

6. The butler _____ that Hector left the house at about 12:00 and returned at 3:15.

7. Elvira de Mendoza _____ that she was at the hairdresser's.

8. The chauffeur _____ the police that he drove Elvira to the hairdresser's at 2:00.

9. The hairdresser _____ that Elvira de Mendoza had an appointment at 2:00, but she didn't show up.

10. The gardener _____ the police that he saw a man arrive at the house at about 2:50.

11. He _____ to the police, "I don't wear a watch, so I can't tell you the exact time."

12. Paco de Mendoza _____ the following story: "I was sleeping in my room. All of a sudden I heard a strange noise in the study."

13. The maid _____ that Paco was in his room from 1:00 to 2:45.

14. One of the police officers said, "I think one member of the family _____ a lie."

15. He also said, "The others probably _____ the truth."

Make It Work

Answer the questions.
Which member of the family told a lie? How do you know?

_____ a lie. _____ told _____

_____ , but _____ .

New Words:

show up—arrive
will—the document that tells what a person wants to happen after his or her death

99

The doctor told her to drink lots of liquids.

IMPERATIVES

INDIRECT SPEECH

GrammarGuide
6.5

The doctor said to Mrs. Murphy, "Relax."

The doctor | told Mrs. Murphy to relax. |

The doctor said to Mrs. Murphy, "Don't worry."

The doctor | told Mrs. Murphy not to worry. |

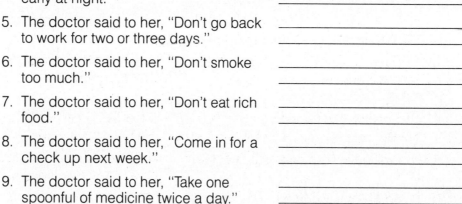

Note: Negatives are formed by placing *not* before the infinitive.

Practice

Mrs. Murphy is sick. This is what the doctor said to Mrs. Murphy.

Change the direct speech to indirect speech.

1. The doctor said to Mrs. Murphy, "Drink lots of liquids."

   The doctor told Mrs. Murphy to drink lots of liquids.

2. The doctor said to Mrs. Murphy, "Don't drink any alcohol."

3. The doctor said to her, "Get lots of rest."

4. The doctor said to her, "Go to bed early at night."

5. The doctor said to her, "Don't go back to work for two or three days."

6. The doctor said to her, "Don't smoke too much."

7. The doctor said to her, "Don't eat rich food."

8. The doctor said to her, "Come in for a check up next week."

9. The doctor said to her, "Take one spoonful of medicine twice a day."

10. The doctor said to her, "Don't worry."

Make It Work

The last time you went to the doctor, what did he or she tell you to do?

The doctor told me to take some medicine.

My fortune says that I will take a trip soon.

STATEMENTS
INDIRECT SPEECH

GrammarGuide
3.10

My fortune says that [I] will take a trip soon.

Bob's fortune says that an old friend will bring [him] good news.

Practice

Change the sentences to indirect speech.

1. You will meet someone new within a week.

   My fortune <u>says that I will meet someone new within a week.</u>

2. You will get married and be happy.

   Dorothy's fortune _____

3. Someone has a pleasant surprise for you.

   Jack's fortune _____

4. You will receive a lot of money.

   My fortune _____

5. You will change your employment soon.

   Gilbert's fortune _____

6. You will receive something new this week.

   My fortune _____

7. An old friend will bring you good news.

   Gloria's fortune _____

8. An unexpected event will bring you money.

   Rafael's fortune _____

9. You will have many pleasures ahead.

   My fortune _____

10. Good news will come to you from far away.

    Oscar's fortune _____

11. You can expect a change in residence soon.

    Dennis' fortune _____

12. You will take a long trip soon.

    Yukiko's fortune _____

New Words:

event—a happening
residence—the place where you live

101

Bill Jones called and said he wouldn't be in today.

STATEMENTS
INDIRECT SPEECH

GrammarGuide
6.5

Bill Jones said, "I don't feel well."   Bill Jones said that | he didn't | feel well.

He said, "I won't be in today."   He said that | he wouldn't | be in today.

Note: When you report another person's words with *said,* change both
the pronouns and verb tense. Present tense usually
changes to past tense: is/am/are → was/were.
Can changes to *could; will* changes to *would.*
The word *that* is optional.

 Practice

Look at each telephone message. Then complete the sentence to report the message.
Use indirect speech.

"Hello. This is Bill Jones. I don't feel well. I won't be in today."

1. Bill Jones called and said that __he didn't feel well_____ .

2. He said _____ .

"Hi. This is Irma Sutter. Tell Mr. Travers I'll be late this morning. I'll be in at 10:30."

3. Irma Sutter called. She said that _____ .

4. She said _____ .

"This is Jim Torpino from Washington. Please have Mr. Travers call me back. It's urgent."

5. Jim Torpino called from Washington. He wants you to call him back. He said that

_____ .

"Good morning. It's Sue from the sales department. Look, I'm very busy today. The
report probably won't be ready until tomorrow."

6. Sue from the sales department called. She said that _____

_____ .

7. She said _____ .

"Saul Jacobs here. I can't come to the meeting today. Will you give him the message?"

8. Saul Jacobs said that _____ .

"This is Alice Snyder. Tell Mr. Travers the meeting this afternoon is canceled."

9. Alice Snyder called and said _____ .

"This is John Woodward. I'll call back later."

10. John Woodward called. He said _____ .

102

Apples are grown in Washington.

SIMPLE PRESENT

PASSIBE VOICE

GrammarGuide
4.26

Apples	are grown	in Washington.
Washington	is known	for its apples.

Note: Use *is, am*, or *are* + the past participle to form the present tense of the passive voice.

Regular participles are formed by adding *d* or *ed* to the simple form of the verb:
plant–planted   use–used

Irregular Past Participles:
grow–grown   sell–sold
know–known   make–made
eat–eaten

Practice

Fill in the blanks with the passive voice.

1. (grow) Apples __are grown__ in New York and California.

2. (know) However, the state of Washington _____ for its apples.

3. (grow) Usually apples _____ in orchards.

4. (plant) Apple trees _____ in rows forty to fifty feet from each other.

5. (cover) In the spring, the apple trees _____ with white flowers.

6. (pick) The apples _____ in the fall.

7. (pack) Then they _____ into crates.

8. (load) The crates _____ onto trucks.

9. (deliver) The best apples _____ to stores.

10. (sell) They _____ at fruit and vegetable stores or in grocery stores.

11. (consume) Millions of apples _____ each year.

12. (make) Apple sauce _____ from some apples.

13. (use) Some _____ for making apple juice.

14. (eat) Others _____ raw.

15. (use) Many _____ for baking.

New Words:

consume–eat or use
orchard–a field or garden where fruit trees grow
crate–a large wooden box
raw–not cooked

103

Where's the report? It's being written now.

PRESENT CONTINUOUS
PASSIVE VOICE

GrammarGuide
4.26

| The letters | are being typed | now. |
| The report | is being written | now. |

Note: Use *am*, *is*, or *are* + *being* + the past participle
to form the present continuous passive voice.

Irregular Past Participles:
make–made
write–written
send–sent

 Practice

Answer the questions. Use the present continuous in the passive voice.

1. Where's the package? (wrap)   It's being wrapped.

2. Where are the letters? (type)   _____

3. Where's the coffee? (make)   _____

4. Where's the mail? (open)   _____

5. Where's the brochure? (print)   _____

6. Where are the sales figures? (add) _____

7. Where are the supplies? (deliver) _____

8. Where's the memo? (copy)   _____

9. Where are the letters? (sign)   _____

10. Where are the checks? (send)   _____

11. Where's my folder? (use)   _____

12. Where's the letter? (write)   _____

The injured people were taken to the hospital.

SIMPLE PAST
PASSIVE VOICE

GrammarGuide
4.27
6.2

> | A truck | was hit | by another truck. |
> | Then the two trucks | were hit | by several other cars. |
>
> **Note:** Use *was* or *were* + the past participle to form the past passive voice.
>
> **Irregular Past Participles:**
> hurt–hurt   take–taken
> hit–hit
> put–put

Practice

Fill in the blanks with the past form of the passive voice.

SIX PEOPLE KILLED IN AUTO ACCIDENT

Tuesday, Dec. 19--Six people __were killed__ in an automobile accident on the
                              (1. kill)

Santa Monica Freeway yesterday. Seventeen other people _____ . Six
                                                              (2. hurt)

trucks and seventeen cars _____ in the accident.
                              (3. involve)

The accident occurred shortly after 8:00 a.m. when a truck _____ by
                                                                 (4. hit)

another truck. Then the two trucks _____ by several other cars. The cars
                                        (5. hit)

and trucks caught fire. Some of the people _____ by other cars when they
                                                (6. injure)

tried to escape the fire. An ambulance _____ to the scene and fire trucks
                                            (7. call)

_____ . Then, the state police _____ . The fire
   (8. notify)   (9. notify)

_____ at about noon yesterday. The injured people _____ to
   (10. put out)   (11. take)

the hospital. The freeway _____ to traffic all day.
                              (12. close)

New Words:

catch fire–start to burn
escape–get away; reach freedom
freeway–highway

105

Her jewelry was taken.

SIMPLE PAST
PASSIVE VOICE

GrammarGuide
4.25
6.2

Someone broke into her house.   **Her house** | was broken | **into.**

Note: Use *was* **and** *were* **+ past participle when you don't know who did the action.**

Irregular Past Participles:
 leave–left   **break–broken**
  steal–stolen   **throw–thrown**

 Practice

Change the sentences to the passive voice.

1. Last Saturday evening, someone robbed Ellen Downing, age 28.

   <u>Last Saturday evening, Ellen Downing, age 28, was robbed.</u>

2. Shortly after midnight, someone broke into her house.

   Shortly after midnight, _____

3. Someone broke the downstairs windows.

4. Someone threw her clothes everywhere.

5. Someone unlocked her jewelry box.

6. Someone took her gold jewelry.

7. Someone stole her stereo and television.

8. Someone took some money.

9. Someone left the front door open.

10. Someone in the neighborhood called the police.

New Word:
break into–to enter a building by force

106

Answers to Exercises

Page 1
2. Cars cost $6,000.
3. Televisions cost $400.
4. Washing machines cost $350.
5. Clothes dryers cost $400.
6. Refrigerators cost $700.
7. Stereos cost $800.
8. Dishwashers cost $500.
9. Stoves cost $800.
10. Beds cost $500.
11. Rugs cost $350.
12. Couches cost $650.

Page 2
2. Serving dishes and salad bowls are in the houseware department.
3. Dressers and chairs are in the furniture department.
4. Shower curtains and bath mats are in the bath department.
5. Sheets and blankets are in the bedding department.
6. Couches and coffee tables are in the furniture department.
7. Pots and pans are in the houseware department.
8. Towels and wash cloths are in the bath department.
9. Televisions and stereos are in the appliance department.
10. Tables and chairs are in the furniture department.
11. Pillow cases and sheets are in the bedding department.
12. Washing machines and clothes dryers are in the appliance department.

Page 3
2. baths
3. bedrooms
4. walls
5. roofs
6. patios
7. garages
8. fireplaces
9. dens
10. studies
11. bookshelves
12. ovens
13. window boxes
14. radios
15. floors

Page 5
2. Goldfish aren't dangerous.
3. Rattlesnakes are dangerous.
4. Alligators are dangerous.
5. Pigeons aren't dangerous.
6. Geese aren't dangerous.
7. Mice aren't dangerous.
8. Rats are dangerous.
9. Deer aren't dangerous.
10. Horses aren't dangerous.
11. Sheep aren't dangerous.
12. Wasps are dangerous.

Page 6
2. A shark is a fish.
3. A snake is a reptile.
4. A butterfly is an insect.
5. A goose is a bird.
6. An alligator is a reptile.
7. A wasp is an insect.
8. A parrot is a bird.
9. A mouse is a rodent.
10. A fly is an insect.
11. A turtle is a reptile.
12. A cockroach is an insect.
13. A rat is a rodent.
14. An ant is an insect.
15. A goldfish is a fish.

Page 7
2. the flower pots
3. the rose bushes
4. the garden tools
5. the beach chairs
6. the paint brushes
7. the salad bowls
8. the coffee tables
9. the shower curtains
10. the office supplies
11. the picture frames
12. the wall clocks

Page 8
3. Another tie
4. Another
5. The other tie
6. The other
7. The other ties
8. The others
9. Another tie
10. Another

Page 9
2. My apartment is also too small.
3. It isn't spacious enough, either.
4. The kitchen isn't large enough.
5. There's one closet in the apartment, and it's too small.
6. It isn't cool enough in the summer.
7. In the winter, it's too cool.
8. It isn't close enough to a shopping area.
9. And it's too far from the bus station.
10. My building isn't elegant enough on the outside.
11. My street isn't safe enough.
12. And the neighborhood is too dangerous.

Page 10

3. He's too small to play on the football team.
4. He isn't big enough to play on the football team.
5. He isn't heavy enough to play on the football team.
6. He's too light to play on the football team.
7. She isn't fast enough to run on the track team.
8. She's too slow to run on the track team.
9. He's too young to play professional baseball.
10. He isn't old enough to play professional baseball.

Page 11

2. There are a lot of jobs in a big city.
3. There are a lot of tall buildings in a big city.
4. There are a lot of big department stores in a big city.
5. There are a lot of museums in a big city.
6. There's a lot of air pollution in a big city.
7. There's a lot of litter in a big city.
8. There are a lot of factories in a big city.
9. There's a lot of noise in a big city.
10. There's a lot of traffic in a big city.
11. There's a lot of crime in a big city.
12. There are a lot of robberies in a big city.

Page 12

2. There isn't much traffic in a small town.
3. There aren't many highways in a small town.
4. There aren't many supermarkets in a small town.
5. There aren't many restaurants in a small town.
6. There isn't much noise at night in a small town.
7. There isn't much crime in a small town.
8. There aren't many apartment buildings in a small town.
9. There isn't much industry in a small town.
10. There aren't many department stores in a small town.
11. There isn't much air pollution in a small town.
12. There aren't many factories in a small town.

Page 13

2. There's no industry in Titusville.
3. There's no air pollution in Titusville.
4. There are no department stores in Titusville.
5. There are no shops in Titusville.
6. There are no supermarkets in Titusville.
7. There's no activity at night in Titusville.
8. There are no highways in Titusville.
9. There's no traffic in Titusville.
10. There are no apartment buildings in Titusville.
11. There are no hotels in Titusville.
12. There's no noise at night in Titusville.
13. There are no restaurants in Titusville.
14. There are no bars in Titusville.
15. There are no movie theaters in Titusville.

Pages 14 and 15

2. I'm teaching
3. she's going
4. is writing
5. isn't working
6. are building
7. They're doing
8. They're working
9. She's studying
10. She's working
11. is getting
12. They're living
13. They're working
14. is building
15. is selling
16. are living
17. aren't doing
18. isn't working
19. is looking
20. they're getting

Page 16

2. Is Tina still teaching?
3. Is LuEllen still going to school?
4. Are Patty and her husband still building a house?
5. Is Mary Lu's husband still writing a novel?
6. Are Dave and Mike Robertson still working for their father?
7. Is Linda Lee still studying at the university?
8. Are Sue and Tom O'Connor still living in Texas?
9. Is Tom O'Connor still building houses?
10. Is Sue O'Connor still selling houses?
11. Are Bill O'Connor and his wife still living in New York?
12. Is Bill O'Connor's wife still looking for a job?

Page 17

2. She produces movies.
3. He drives taxis.
4. She washes windows.
5. She makes dresses.
6. She operates switchboards.
7. He trains animals.
8. He publishes books.
9. She drives trucks.
10. He makes shoes.
11. He paints houses.
12. She keeps books.
13. He catches dogs.
14. She tunes pianos.
15. He cleans streets.

Page 18
2. gets
3. clean
4. cleans
5. fix
6. fixes
7. answer
8. answers
9. get
10. helps
11. answer
12. answers

Page 19
2. They're tellers who handle a lot of money every day.
3. They cash checks for people.
4. They add figures, and they count money.
5. They count everything twice so that they don't make mistakes.
6. Their jobs require a lot of accuracy.
7. They also have to be fast at what they do.
8. They receive and pay out hundreds of dollars every hour.
9. They smile at all the customers.
10. They enjoy their jobs very much.
11. But there's one thing that worries them.
12. They're afraid of bank robbers.

Page 20
2. on
3. at
4. in
5. in/in
6. on
7. in
8. on/in
9. in/on
10. at
11. on
12. in/at

Page 21
2. in
3. in
4. on
5. on
6. on
7. at
8. at
9. in
10. on
11. in
12. on
13. at
14. on
15. at

Page 22
2. What time in the evening does he arrive?
3. What time on Friday do they leave?
4. What time on Wednesday does it leave?
5. What time on March 18th does she arrive?
6. What time in the morning do you arrive?
7. What time on February 6th do you arrive?
8. What time on Sunday do they arrive?
9. What time on the 9th do you leave?
10. What time in the morning does it arrive?
11. What time on September 6th do they leave?
12. What time in the afternoon does he leave?

Page 23
Suggested answers:
2. to become (to be)
3. to go (to travel)
4. to earn (to save)
5. to go (to travel)
6. to get
7. to get
8. to work (to try)
9. to become (to be)
10. to give up

Page 24
2. signing
3. getting
4. having
5. being
6. making
7. doing
8. making
9. rehearsing
10. talking

Page 25
2. to take
3. working
4. to go
5. working
6. having
7. to be
8. to give up
9. staying
10. working
11. being
12. to be

Page 26
Answers beginning with:
I don't know
I'm not sure
I have no idea
3. I have no idea what she wants.
4. I'm not sure what her favorite color is.
5. I have no idea what kind of book she likes.
6. I don't know what type of jewelry she likes.
7. I'm not sure what glove size she wears.
8. I don't know what her favorite perfume is.
9. I have no idea what kind of candy she likes.
10. I don't know what her favorite flower is.

Page 27

2. Do you know what time it starts?
3. Do you know what time the next show starts?
4. Do you know where it's (it is) playing?
5. Do you know where the Strand Theater is?
6. Do you know how far it is?
7. Do you know how long it takes to get there?
8. Do you know what time it ends?
9. Do you know how long it is?
10. Do you know how much it costs?

Page 29

2. decided
3. baked
4. packed
5. walked
6. stopped
7. picked
8. jumped
9. followed
10. asked
11. answered
12. liked
13. arrived
14. noticed
15. entered

Page 30

2. lived
3. live
4. visit
5. live
6. walked
7. jumped
8. followed
9. stop
10. talk
11. wanted
12. trick
13. like
14. liked
15. knock
16. walked
17. see
18. expected
19. kill
20. killed

Page 31

2. interesting
3. frightening
4. frightened
5. confusing
6. confused
7. shocked
8. shocking
9. entertained
10. entertaining
11. fascinating
12. fascinated
13. surprised
14. surprising
Make It Work
interesting (entertaining)
boring (confusing)
surprised
confused (bored)

Page 33

2. She attended Huntington Elementary School from 1950 to 1958.
3. She attended Huntington Elementary School for eight years.
4. She completed the eighth (8th) grade.
5. She attended high school for four years.
6. She went to Newport High School.
7. She attended Newport High School from 1959 to 1963.
8. She completed the twelfth (12th) grade.
9. She received a diploma.
10. She graduated from Newport High School.
11. She went to the University of California.
12. Her major subject was English.
13. She attended the University of California from 1964 to 1968.
14. She received a bachelor's degree.
15. She graduated from the University of California.

Page 35

2. He was an English teacher.
3. He taught English.
4. He worked for Greenfield High School for eleven years.
5. He earned $14,500.
6. He left Greenfield High School because he got a job in California.
7. He worked for Ames Department Store.
8. He was a sales clerk.
9. He sold furniture.
10. He worked for Ames Department Store from 1968 to 1970.
11. He earned $7,000.
12. He left Ames Department Store because he got a teaching job in Massachusetts.

Page 36

2. How long did you work for Star Shoe Company?
3. When did she leave A.B.C. Company?
4. Why did she leave A.B.C. Company?
5. When were you a secretary?
6. How much did you earn at Selby Company?
7. How long did she work for a bank?
8. Who did she work for?
9. When did you go to Harbor High School?
10. How long did you go to Harbor High School?
11. When did he graduate from college?
12. What college did he graduate from?

Page 37

2. screamed
3. started
4. saw
5. chased
6. ran
7. hit
8. came
9. heard
10. began
11. joined
12. caught
13. found
14. heard
15. called

Page 38

Individual answers.
See irregular past tense verbs at the top of the page.

Page 39

2. made
3. did
4. did
5. did
6. did
7. made
8. made
9. did
10. do
11. did
12. did
13. do
14. made
15. did

Page 40

2. She mailed her grandmother a gift.
3. She bought her family gifts.
4. She got her children toys.
5. She gave her father a book.
6. She ordered her mother flowers.
7. She made her sister an apron.
8. She baked her aunt and uncle some cookies.
9. She got her husband a tie.
10. She cooked her family a big meal.
11. She served everyone turkey.
12. She read her children a story.

Page 41

2. The wine steward brought some wine to them.
3. He poured some wine for Mr. Green.
4. After Mr. Green tasted it, he poured some wine for Mr. Bang.
5. Then the waiter handed menus to them.
6. Mr. Green gave their order to the waiter.
7. He ordered steak for them.
8. After fifteen or twenty minutes, the waiter brought their food to them.
9. After dinner, the waiter served coffee and dessert to them.
10. When the meal was over, the waiter handed the check to Mr. Green.
11. Mr. Green gave some money to the waiter.
12. He also left a tip for the waiter.

Page 42

2. for
3. ---
4. ---
5. for
6. ---
7. to
8. to
9. for
10. ---
11. to
12. ---
13. to
14. ---
15. for

Page 43

2. She picked a black suit out.
3. She took her sweater off.
4. She tried the jacket on, but it didn't fit.
5. Then she picked a gray suit out.
6. The jacket fit perfectly. She went to the dressing room and put the skirt on.
7. The skirt fit, so she hung the suit up.
8. Then she took the suit to the cash register. She made a check out for $149.29.
9. She wrote her telephone number down on the back of the check.
10. The clerk folded the suit up and put it into a box.
11. Lois picked the box up and left the store.
12. She thought, "I can always take the suit back if I change my mind."

Page 44

2. I put them on.
3. I picked it up.
4. I looked it over.
5. I wrote them down.
6. I filled them in.
7. I looked them up in the dictionary.
8. I read it over.
9. I crossed them out.
10. I handed it in.

Make It Work

I looked it over before I began to write.
When I was finished, I read it over.
I handed it in on time.

Page 45

2. was cleaning
3. were running
4. were playing
5. were sleeping
6. was listening
7. were studying
8. was watching
9. was taking
10. were eating

Page 46

2. He was talking on the telephone when the accident happened.
3. He was watching television when Steve came over.
4. He was relaxing on the patio when it began to rain.
5. He was taking a nap when his alarm clock accidentally went off.
6. He was cooking dinner when the baby cried.
7. He was eating dinner when he heard a loud noise.
8. He was studying when the doorbell rang.
9. He was taking a bath when Mary called.
10. He was reading a book when the dog started to bark.

Page 47

2. She hurt her back while she was moving furniture.
3. He cut his finger while he was cooking.
4. I fell down while I was riding a bicycle.
5. He slipped while he was walking in the snow.
6. She bumped her head while she was getting out of the car.
7. He tore his pants while he was working in the yard.
8. I burned my hand while I was cooking.
9. They had an accident while they were driving.
10. He broke his leg while he was playing football.

Page 48

2. cut/was shaving
3. was taking/rang
4. was taking/slipped/fell
5. rang/was making
6. was talking/began
7. was making/knocked
8. was frying/burned
9. broke/was doing
10. decided/went

Page 49

2. They've cleaned up their rooms once so far.
3. She's cooked dinner four nights so far.
4. He's watered the plants once so far.
5. She's vacuumed the rug once so far.
6. They've cleaned the bathroom once this week.
7. He's dusted the furniture twice this week.
8. He's cooked dinner once so far.
9. She's ironed the clothes once so far.
10. They've changed the beds twice so far.

Page 50

2. He hasn't taken out the trash since Wednesday.
3. They haven't cleaned up their rooms since Tuesday.
4. She hasn't fed the dog since yesterday.
5. She hasn't washed the clothes since Wednesday.
6. She hasn't ironed the clothes since Monday.
7. They haven't done the dishes since yesterday.
8. He hasn't watered the plants since Tuesday.
9. He hasn't paid the bills since last month.
10. She hasn't vacuumed the rug since Thursday.

Page 51

3. for
4. since
5. for
6. since
7. since
8. for
9. since
10. for
11. for
12. since
13. since
14. for
15. since

Page 52

2. Have you turned off the lights?
3. Have you left an outside light on?
4. Have you closed the windows?
5. Have you pulled down the shades?
6. Have you taken out the trash?
7. Have you put out your cigarette?
8. Have you made sure the oven is off?
9. Have you fed the cat?
10. Have you taken your keys with you?
11. Have you taken your money with you?
12. Have you locked all the doors?

Page 53

2. How many times has she fed the dog today?
3. How many times have they cleaned up their rooms this week?
4. How many times has she cooked dinner this week?
5. How many times has he washed the car this month?
6. How many times have they cleaned the bathroom this week?
7. How many times has he taken out the trash this week?
8. How many times has she ironed the clothes this month?
9. How many times have they changed the beds this month?
10. How many times has he dusted the furniture this week?

Page 54
2. He's already gotten a passport.
3. He's already seen a travel agent.
4. He's already sent his itinerary to his parents.
5. He's already had his suit cleaned.
6. He's already gone to the bank.
7. He's already bought traveler's checks.
8. He's already gotten travel insurance.
9. He's already made his hotel reservations.
10. He's already paid for his tickets.
11. He's already packed his suitcase.
12. He's already left.

Page 55
2. yet/already
3. yet/yet
4. already/yet
5. already
6. already/yet
7. yet/already
8. already/yet
9. yet
10. yet/already

Page 56
3. Yes, they have.
4. Yes, he has.
5. No, he hasn't.
6. Yes, he has.
7. Yes, he has.
8. Yes, they have.
9. No, he hasn't.
10. No, he hasn't.
11. No, they haven't.
12. No, he hasn't.
13. Yes, he has.
14. No, they haven't.
15. No, they haven't.

Page 57
Individual negative or affirmative answers:
2. Yes, I do. No, I don't.
3. Yes, I have. No, I haven't.
4. Yes, I do. No, I don't.
   Yes, I have. No, I haven't.
5. Yes, I do. No, I don't.
   Yes, I have. No, I haven't.
6. Yes, I have. No, I haven't.
7. Yes, I do. No, I don't.
8. Yes, I have. No, I haven't.
9. Yes, I do. No, I don't.
10. Yes, I do. No, I don't.

Page 59
4. She's been
5. works
6. works
7. started
8. She's worked
9. worked
10. worked
11. lived
12. lives
13. She's lived
14. She's lived
15. worked
16. worked
17. lived
18. was
19. lived
20. worked

Page 60
3. The gray cat is as clean as the black cat.
4. The gray cat isn't as tall as the black cat.
5. The gray cat isn't as playful as the black cat.
6. The gray cat is as long as the black cat.
7. The gray cat is as graceful as the black cat.
8. The gray cat is as gentle as the black cat.
9. The gray cat isn't as friendly as the black cat.
10. The gray cat isn't as heavy as the black cat.
11. The gray cat is as active as the black cat.
12. The gray cat isn't as beautiful as the black cat.

Page 61
2. more modern
3. sunnier
4. noisier
5. closer
6. smaller
7. more expensive
8. smaller
9. more beautiful
10. larger
11. more spacious
12. prettier

Page 63
2. faster than Carole
3. more politely than Bruce
4. more carefully than Bruce
5. more accurately than Carole
6. earlier than Bruce
7. later than Carole
8. harder than Bruce
9. more quickly than Carole
10. more carefully than Bruce
11. more neatly than Bruce
12. more easily than Carole

Page 64
Suggested answers:
3. Eat more yogurt.
4. Eat less candy.
5. Eat less sugar.
6. Eat more carrots.
7. Drink less alcohol.
8. Eat more eggs.
9. Eat fewer potato chips.
10. Drink more milk.
11. Drink less coffee.
12. Eat fewer cookies.
13. Eat more apples.
14. Drink fewer soft drinks.
15. Eat less cake.

Page 65
2. Alberta is taller than Olga is.
3. Alberta is older than Olga.
4. Alberta dresses more neatly than Olga does.
5. Alberta is more friendly than Olga is.
6. Alberta is nicer than Olga is.
7. Alberta gets along with people more easily than Olga.
8. Alberta plays tennis better than Olga does.
9. Alberta is more intelligent than Olga is.
10. Alberta reads more books than Olga does.

Page 66
2. My gloves are the same as yours.
3. My camera is the same as yours.
4. My umbrella is different from yours.
5. My ring is different from yours.
6. My watch is the same as yours.
7. My slacks are the same as yours.
8. My scarf is different from yours.
9. My coat is the same as yours.
10. My shirt is different from yours.
11. My wallet is different from yours.
12. My pen is the same as yours.

Page 67
2. the most elegant
3. the most expensive
4. the slowest
5. the best
6. the most delicious
7. the most crowded
8. the fastest
9. the friendliest
10. the cheapest

Page 69
2. the earliest
3. the latest
4. the latest
5. the closest
6. the farthest
7. the most carefully
8. the most quickly
9. the best
10. the most easily

Page 70
2. A cat is bigger than a mouse, but a horse is the biggest of the three.
3. A cat is smaller than a dog, but a mouse is the smallest of the three.
4. A scorpion is more dangerous than a snake, but a shark is the most dangerous of the three.
5. A cat is friendlier than a horse, but a dog is the friendliest of the three.
6. A dog is stronger than a cat, but a horse is the strongest of the three.
7. A cat is more graceful than a dog, but a bird is the most graceful of the three.
8. A turtle is slower than an ant, but a snail is the slowest of the three.
9. A dog is faster than a cat, but a horse is the fastest of the three.
10. A butterfly is more colorful than a moth, but a parrot is the most colorful of the three.

Page 71
2. will be
3. will start
4. will walk
5. She'll wear
6. She'll stand
7. will leave
8. will throw
9. will be
10. will drink
11. will cut
12. they'll dance
13. will leave
14. They'll get
15. they'll drive

Page 72
2. Nick's aunt will reserve the church.
3. She'll also make the wedding dress.
4. Andrea's cousin will make a wedding cake.
5. Andrea's parents will have the reception at their house.
6. Nick's parents will give a party too.
7. Andrea's brother will sing a song.
8. He'll also play the piano.
9. Andrea's father will read a poem.
10. Nick's brother will drive them to the reception.
11. He'll also take photos.
12. Andrea's grandmother will serve the champagne.

Page 73
2. will look/walks
3. is/will leave
4. will take/leave
5. leave/will throw
6. arrive/will drink
7. dance/will dance
8. will throw/leave
9. will be
10. throws/will get

Page 74
2. After she sees London, she'll fly to Paris.
3. When she's (she is) in Paris, she'll see the Cathedral of Notre Dame.
4. After she leaves Paris, she'll go to Rome.
5. When she visits Rome, she'll go to some museums.
6. When she's (she is) in Rome, she'll see a lot of famous fountains.
7. After she sees Rome, she'll go to Madrid.
8. After she spends a day in Madrid, she'll go to Athens.
9. When she visits Athens, she'll see some famous statues.
10. After she leaves Athens, she'll fly back to Tokyo.

Page 75

3. the
4. ---
5. ---
6. the
7. ---
8. ---
9. the
10. ---
11. the
12. ---

Page 76

2. Roy and Becky won't do their homework.
3. Roy won't take out the trash.
4. Becky won't practice the piano.
5. Roy won't feed the dog.
6. Roy and Becky won't turn off the television set.
7. Becky won't set the table.
8. Becky won't put the soda back in the refrigerator.
9. Roy won't eat everything on his plate.
10. Roy and Becky won't do the dishes.

Page 77

2. yourself
3. myself
4. themselves
5. himself
6. herself
7. themselves
8. themselves
9. yourselves
10. ourselves

Page 78

Individual answers beginning with:
I'd take . . .   or
I wouldn't take . . .

Page 79

Individual answers, beginning with:
If I were . . .

Page 80

Individual answers. Some suggested answers are:
2. If I needed money, I'd call my father (a friend).
3. If I had a headache, I'd take some aspirin.
4. If I felt sick, I'd go to bed.
5. If I broke my arm, I'd call a doctor (the hospital).
6. If my house were on fire, I'd call the fire department.
7. If I saw a car accident, I'd call an ambulance (the police department).
8. If someone robbed my house (or apartment), I'd call the police.
9. If I lost the keys to my house (or apartment), I'd call my husband (or wife). (I'd climb in through the window.)
10. If someone stole my wallet, I'd call the police.

Page 81

3. You should plan your meals in advance.
4. You should use coupons.
5. You shouldn't buy fresh fruit and vegetables out of season.
6. You should compare the prices of several brands.
7. You should buy store brands.
8. You should buy large boxes and cans.
9. You shouldn't buy a lot of processed food.
10. You shouldn't buy more fresh food than you need.
11. You should keep food carefully.
12. You shouldn't buy food you don't want just because it's on sale.
13. You should check the expiration date on dairy products.
14. You should buy frozen food last.
15. You shouldn't shop on an empty stomach.

Page 82

3. He'd better not leave his wallet on the counter.
4. He'd better put his wallet away.
5. She'd better not leave her door unlocked.
6. She'd better lock the door.
7. She'd better not walk home late at night.
8. She'd better take a taxi.
9. He'd better not leave his camera in the car.
10. He'd better take his camera with him.
11. She'd better not leave the windows open.
12. She'd better close (lock) the windows.

Page 83

3. have to be
4. must check in
5. have to reserve
6. must check
7. have to get
8. have to go
9. must wait
10. must show
11. have to sit
12. must fasten

Page 84

2. don't have to
3. don't have to
4. must not
5. must not
6. don't have to
7. must not
8. don't have to
9. don't have to
10. must not

Page 85

2. He must be a doctor.
3. She must be a police officer.
4. He must be a painter.
5. He must be a boxer.
6. She must be a waitress.
7. She must be a business executive.
8. He must be a musician.
9. She must be a dancer.
10. He must be a carpenter.

Page 86

2. He might have something else to do tonight.
3. He might not know that the party is tonight.
4. He might be sick.
5. He might not know what time the party starts.
6. He might not know the address.
7. He might be lost.
8. He might not know how to get here.
9. He might be in a traffic jam.
10. He might be in trouble.

Page 87

2. He'd rather eat at home.
3. Karen would rather not eat at home.
4. She'd rather not cook dinner.
5. She'd rather eat at a restaurant.
6. Charlie would rather eat Italian food.
7. Karen would rather not eat Italian food.
8. She'd rather eat Chinese food.
9. She'd rather eat at Ming's.
10. Charlie would rather eat at The Great Wall.
11. Karen would rather not watch television at home.
12. She'd rather go to a movie.
13. Charlie would rather not go to a movie.
14. He'd rather go home after dinner.
15. He'd rather watch television.

Page 88

Individual answers.
2. No, I wouldn't. Yes, I would.
3. I'd rather eat French food. I'd rather eat Italian food.
4. I'd rather have steak. I'd rather have pizza.
5. Yes, I would. No, I wouldn't.
6. I'd rather go to a fancy restaurant. I'd rather go to a casual restaurant.
7. Yes, I would. No, I wouldn't.
8. I'd rather go somewhere. I'd rather stay at home.
9. No, I wouldn't. Yes, I would.
10. I'd rather go to a movie. I'd rather watch television.

Page 89

2. can't
3. won't
4. is
5. must
6. will
7. am
8. did
9. was
10. would

Page 90

2. They had to wash all the windows.
3. They had to put in screens
4. They had to fix the stove.
5. They had to buy a refrigerator.
6. They had to build a counter in the kitchen.
7. They had to paint the inside of the house.
8. They had to fix the roof.
9. They had to buy an air conditioner.
10. They had to put in light fixtures.

Page 91

2. He didn't have to buy a refrigerator.
3. He didn't have to buy a stove.
4. He didn't have to build a counter in the kitchen.
5. He didn't have to paint the inside of the house.
6. He didn't have to fix the roof.
7. He didn't have to put in light fixtures.
8. He didn't have to buy new rugs.
9. He didn't have to put in an air conditioner.
10. He didn't have to wash the windows.

Page 92

2. He could play tennis all day ten years ago.
3. He could read without his glasses ten years ago.
4. He could go out every night ten years ago.
5. He could stay up all night ten years ago.
6. He could run up and down the stairs ten years ago.
7. He could lift heavy objects ten years ago.
8. He could eat rich food ten years ago.
9. He could work for twelve hours a day ten years ago.
10. He could run a mile in fifteen minutes ten years ago.

Page 93

2. couldn't go
3. had to walk
4. couldn't buy
5. had to buy
6. couldn't use
7. had to take
8. couldn't use
9. had to use
10. couldn't watch
11. couldn't cook
12. had to eat

Page 94

2. She used to live with her parents.
3. She used to play with dolls.
4. She used to wear cowboy hats and blue jeans.
5. She used to dress up in her mother's clothes.
6. She used to climb trees.
7. She used to play baseball in the street.
8. She used to collect stamps.
9. She used to take ballet lessons.
10. She used to read comic books.

Page 95

2. You didn't use to drink coffee.
3. You didn't use to smoke a lot.
4. You didn't use to like to be alone.
5. You didn't use to read a lot.
6. You didn't use to wear glasses.
7. You didn't use to enjoy classical music.
8. You didn't use to like concerts.
9. You didn't use to like modern art.
10. You didn't use to enjoy serious discussions.
11. You didn't use to like foreign films.
12. You didn't use to like to study.

Page 96

A boy went into a bakery and said to the clerk, "I'd like a loaf of bread, please."

The clerk gave him a loaf of bread. Then he said, "That'll be seventy-five cents, please."

"This is a very small loaf for seventy-five cents," the boy said.

"Perhaps you are right," the clerk said, "but now you won't have so much to carry home." He laughed and held his hand out for the money.

"That's true," the boy replied. He gave the clerk fifty cents and went to the door.

"Hey, stop!" the man shouted. "This isn't enough money!"

"Perhaps you are right," the boy said, "but now you won't have so much to count."

Page 97

2. a/the
3. the/The
4. the/a
5. a/the
6. the/a
7. the/The
8. the
9. the/The/the
10. a/the
11. the/the
12. the/a

Page 99

2. told
3. said
4. told
5. told
6. said
7. said
8. told
9. said
10. told
11. said
12. told
13. said
14. told
15. told

Make It Work

Elvira de Mendoza told a lie. She told the police that she was at the hairdresser's, but the hairdresser said that she didn't show up.

Page 100

2. The doctor told her not to drink any alcohol.
3. The doctor told her to get lots of rest.
4. The doctor told her to go to bed early at night.
5. The doctor told her not to go back to work for two or three days.
6. The doctor told her not to smoke too much.
7. The doctor told her not to eat rich food.
8. The doctor told her to come in for a check-up next week.
9. The doctor told her to take one spoonful of medicine twice a day.
10. The doctor told her not to worry.

Page 101

2. Dorothy's fortune says that she will get married and be happy.
3. Jack's fortune says that someone has a pleasant surprise for him.
4. My fortune says that I will receive a lot of money.
5. Gilbert's fortune says that he will change his employment soon.
6. My fortune says that I will receive something new this week.
7. Gloria's fortune says that an old friend will bring her good news.
8. Rafael's fortune says that an unexpected event will bring him money.
9. My fortune says that I will have many pleasures ahead.
10. Oscar's fortune says that good news will come to him from far away.
11. Dennis' fortune says that he can expect a change in residence soon.
12. Yukiko's fortune says that she will take a long trip soon.

Page 102

2. He said (that) he wouldn't be in today.
3. She said (that) she'd (she would) be late this morning.
4. She said (that) she'd (she would) be in at 10:30.
5. He said (that) it was urgent.
6. She said (that) she was very busy today.
7. She said (that) the report probably wouldn't be ready until tomorrow.
8. Saul Jacobs said (that) he couldn't come to the meeting.
9. Alice Snyder called and said (that) the meeting this afternoon was canceled.
10. He said (that) he'd (he would) call back later.

Page 103
2. is known
3. are grown
4. are planted
5. are covered
6. are picked
7. are packed
8. are loaded
9. are delivered
10. are sold
11. are consumed
12. is made
13. are used
14. are eaten
15. are used

Page 104
2. They're being typed.
3. It's being made.
4. It's being opened.
5. It's being printed.
6. They're being added.
7. They're being delivered.
8. It's being copied.
9. They're being signed.
10. They're being sent.
11. It's being used.
12. It's being written.

Page 105
2. were hurt
3. were involved
4. was hit
5. were hit
6. were injured
7. was called
8. were notified
9. were notified
10. was put out
11. were taken
12. was closed

Page 106
2. Shortly after midnight, her house was broken into.
3. The downstairs windows were broken.
4. Her clothes were thrown everywhere.
5. Her jewelry box was unlocked.
6. Her gold jewelry was taken.
7. Her stereo and television were stolen.
8. Some money was taken.
9. The front door was left open.
10. The police were called.

118